THE MAKING OF THE MODERN GULF STATES: KUWAIT, BAHRAIN, QATAR, THE UNITED ARAB EMIRATES AND OMAN

Rosemarie Said Zahlan

LONDON
UNWIN HYMAN
BOSTON   SYDNEY   WELLINGTON

Published by the Academic Division of

Unwin Hyman Ltd
15/17 Broadwick Street, London W1V 1FP, UK

Unwin Hyman Inc.,
8 Winchester Place, Winchester, Mass. 01890, USA

Allen & Unwin (Australia) Ltd,
8 Napier Street, North Sydney, NSW 2060, Australia

Allen & Unwin (New Zealand) Ltd in association with the Port
Nicholson Press Ltd,
60 Cambridge Terrace, Wellington, New Zealand

First published in 1989

British Library Cataloguing in Publication Data

Zahlan, Rosemarie Said
    The making of the modern Gulf States:
    Kuwait, Bahrain, Qatar, the United Arab
    Emirates and Oman.
    1. Arabia. Gulf States, 1926–
    I. Title
    953′.605
    ISBN 0–04–445293–4

Printed in Great Britain by
Billing and Sons Ltd, London and Worcester

Contents

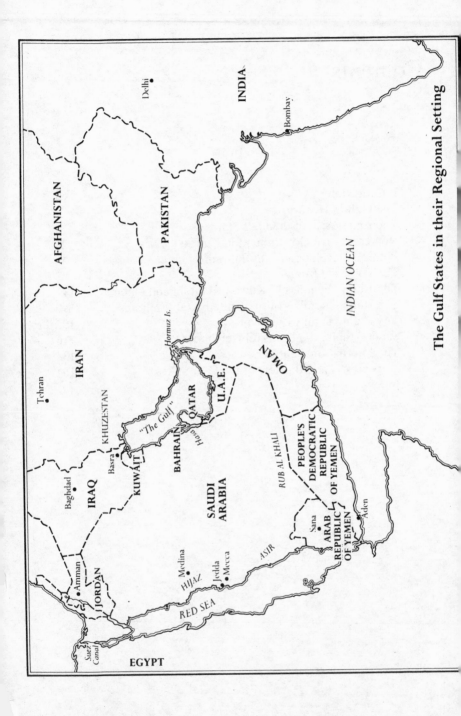

The Gulf States in their Regional Setting

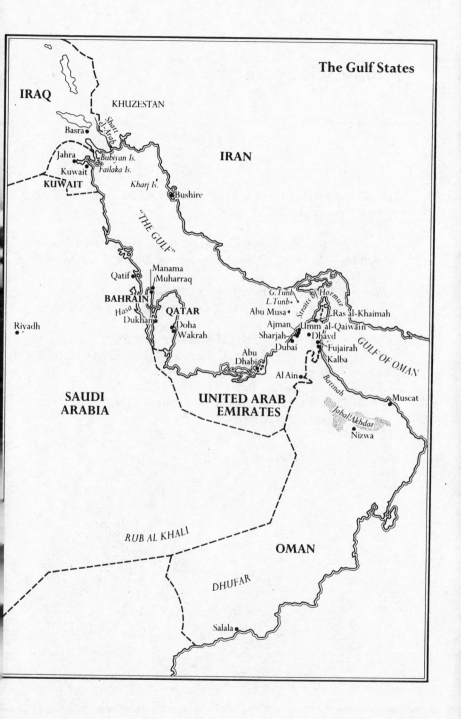

The Gulf States

IRAQ

KHUZESTAN

Basra

Shatt al Arab

Jahra
Kuwait
Bubiyan Is.
Failaka Is.
KUWAIT

IRAN

Kharj Is.
Bushire

"THE GULF"

Qatif
Manama
Muharraq

BAHRAIN
Hasa
Dukhan
QATAR
Doha
Wakrah

G. Tunb
L. Tunb
Abu Musa

Straits of Hormuz

Ras al-Khaimah

Ajman
Sharjah
Umm al-Qaiwain
Dubai
Dhayd
Fujairah
Kalba

GULF OF OMAN

Riyadh

Abu Dhabi

Al Ain

Batinah

Muscat

SAUDI ARABIA

UNITED ARAB EMIRATES

Jabal Akhdar
Nizwa

RUB AL KHALI

OMAN

DHUFAR

Salala

Acknowledgements

The photographs in this book are reproduced by courtesy of the following copyright holders.

Photo 1: From the Freya Stark Collection, Middle East Centre, St Antony's College, Oxford; by permission of John Murray (Publishers) Ltd.
Photo 2: Bernard Gerard/The Hutchinson Library.
Photo 3: From the Slade Baker Collection, Middle East Centre, St Antony's College.
Photo 4: Peter Hellyer/The Hutchinson Library.
Photo 5: From the Bowman Collection, Middle East Centre, St Antony's College.
Photo 6: Tim Graham Picture Library.
Photo 7: Robin Constable/The Hutchinson Library.
Photos 8 and 9: Jill Brown.

Introduction

Until the 1970s, the five Gulf states (Kuwait, Bahrain, Qatar, the United Arab Emirates, and Oman) were hardly known beyond the shores of the Gulf. Since then, they have been propelled into the international limelight, this extraordinary transition being marked by a wide variety of misconceptions in the West, where their great wealth evoked images of extravagance, medieval splendour and autocratic rule.

These early misconceptions gradually faded as an awareness of the realities of the Gulf region grew. Nevertheless, the Gulf states today remain the focus of widespread interest, both because of their strategic location and their principal resource, oil. The states have much in common. They are sparsely populated and most have an overwhelmingly large expatriate community. They are young states; two of them (Qatar and the United Arab Emirates) ended their treaty relations with Britain – a euphemism for attaining independence – as recently as 1971.

By and large, the states are extremely wealthy, in striking contrast to the poverty of only a few decades ago. In 1985, for example, the United Arab Emirates' *per capita* income of $19,270 was the highest in the world, according to the World Bank; a mere thirty years earlier, the economy there was at subsistence level. The high rate of socio-economic change, the rapid expansion of educational and health facilities, the huge development projects, the complex new industries and the sophisticated communications networks that exist there now all attest to the swift transformation taking place.

This transformation relies heavily on international transactions for the provision of the manpower and technology vital to effect it. A state of interdependence has arisen between the Gulf states, the West and Japan. The Gulf states rely on Japan and the West as markets for their oil and as sources for technical services and industrial products, while Japan and the West rely heavily on the Gulf states not only for their energy supplies but also for their financial assets, and the employment opportunities afforded by their rich markets.

This interdependence has given rise to repeated expressions of concern, particularly in the West, about the internal stability of the Gulf states, and their external security. Central to this concern is the knowledge that half the world's proven oil reserves are in the Gulf region, which is also known to possess the greatest potential for further discoveries. It is largely because of these facts that the fleets of so many nations are at present crowding the waters of the Gulf.

The genesis of much of this concern was Britain's termination of its east of Suez defence policy and departure from the Gulf in 1971. It was sharpened by a number of subsequent events: the oil embargo following the 1973 Arab–Israeli war and the consequent dramatic rise in oil prices; the fall of the Pahlavi dynasty and the establishment of the Islamic republic in Iran; and the war between Iraq and Iran which threatened at times to spread beyond the confines of these two countries.

Since the early 1970s, the United States of America (USA) has regarded the Gulf region as vital to its national security interests. While the Pahlavi dynasty was still in power, it relied on the Shah of Iran to act as 'policeman' of the region. After the Islamic revolution in Iran, the USA abruptly and dramatically lost its best friend in the Gulf, leaving it to manifest its policies primarily on the military plane.

Over thirty countries entered the region by supplying either Iraq or Iran – or both, in some cases – with the military supplies vital to the conduct of the war between them. Furthermore, the Soviet occupation of Afghanistan brought the possibility of a superpower confrontation in the Gulf uncomfortably close, as did the decisions taken by the two superpowers to protect shipping in Gulf waters.

The recent oil glut has forced down the respective incomes of the Gulf states, bringing about a recession which has had an inevitable impact on their internal affairs. Expatriates have started to return to their home countries, the construction boom of the past two decades has slowed down visibly, and deficits in the national budgets are being declared. These developments have brought with them a renewed political awareness and a desire to reduce the dependence on foreigners.

In the face of both mounting international tensions and the economic recession, the Gulf states appear to be fragile and unable to withstand the many pressures on them. Moreover, the fabric of their respective societies is often regarded as having been hastily put together in order to participate in the vast wealth bestowed on it.

Because the changes in the Gulf states have been so swift and dramatic, observers have tended to overlook important features which have persisted there despite the many visible transformations taking place in recent years. Indeed, these states have retained many of their past forms of socio-political organization while at the same time undergoing a dramatically high rate of social and economic change.

An understanding of the complexities of the Gulf states requires an examination of the issues, events and personalities which have dominated them. The purpose of this book is to provide the non-specialist reader with a coherent account of those factors which have contributed to the socio-economic and political development of the Gulf states.

A definition of the term 'Gulf states' is necessary in order to avoid confusion. Two categories of states are generally referred to as Gulf states. First, there are the regional powers of Iraq, Iran and Saudi Arabia. Second, there are the small states of Kuwait, Bahrain, Qatar and the United Arab Emirates (UAE). In this book, these small states will be referred to as Gulf states. The Sultanate of Oman falls between the two categories. During the nineteenth century, it was a regional power, but is no longer. The regional powers will be brought into the discussion only in cases where either their specific characteristics or their influence – or both – extend into the region as a whole.

The population of the Gulf states has swollen beyond all recognition in the last three or four decades from the influx of expatriates. Today the population is around 4.62 million, and of these an estimated *2.7 million* (i.e. more than half) are foreigners who have gone there to work, generally for a limited period. The nationals of Kuwait, Qatar and the UAE are now a minority in their own countries.

No analysis of the current situation would be complete without an understanding of the tribal nature of Gulf societies. Until the

very recent past, the tribal structure of the population dominated
political and social life. The modern institutions which have been
established since independence have been adapted to the
traditional forms.

The tribal society of the Gulf states consisted of the bedouin
(*bedu*) and the settled people (*hadar*). The *bedu* roamed the
inland areas in search of grazing and water, while the *hadar* settled
the coastal villages and towns and became the overwhelming
majority. Because of the paramount importance of the sea in the
political economies of the states, the *hadar* came to dominate
economic and political life.

The leader of a tribe is known as a *shaikh*. The ruler of every
state, with the exception of Oman, was also known as the *shaikh*
of that state which was referred to as a *shaikhdom*. After independence, the ruler became known as the *Amir* (Prince) with the
qualification of Highness; and the members of his family have the
title of *Shaikh* (*Shaikhah*, feminine). The Sultan of Oman has
held the same title since the nineteenth century and is known by
it today, with the added qualification of Majesty; the members of
his family have the title of *Sayyid* (*Sayyidah*, feminine).

The position of Gulf women has been the subject of considerable misinterpretation in the West. Because some are heavily
shrouded in veils, visions are inevitably conjured of a state of
eternal seclusion. But, despite outward appearances, Gulf women
traditionally enjoy considerably more involvement in day-to-day
activity than many of their sisters elsewhere in the Arab world.
The mobility of bedouin life has always been such that women
have had a direct and active role to play in community affairs.
After the bedouin settled the different coastal towns and villages
of the Gulf, their women attained an even higher level of participation. The economies of the Gulf states became dominated by
the pearling industry which employed most of the able-bodied
men. Since the pearling boats stayed at sea for up to four months
at a stretch during the season, the women who remained behind
inevitably moved forward to assume greater responsibility. Many
of their daughters and granddaughters today continue in the same
tradition.

Two principal themes recur throughout this book. The first is
the overwhelming influence of the past on current events in the
Gulf states. Because so much has been eradicated so swiftly as a
result of the windfall of oil revenues, and because the present is

so radically different from the past in outward appearance, it is difficult to perceive much political continuity, but an astonishing amount is there, nevertheless, as the text will reveal.

The second theme is the paramount importance of international forces in the creation and shaping of the modern Gulf states. It would be difficult to find another group of states which owe so much of their political and economic development to external events. Very often these events have been beyond the control of the states, but it has been their ability to contain them and/or to use them to their advantage which has contributed so much to their modern existence.

Chapter 1 places the Gulf region in its historical perspective. Chapter 2 singles out the three most important influences on the emergence of the modern Gulf states: the relationship with Britain; the arrival of the oil companies; and the position of the ruler. In social and political terms, Kuwait and Bahrain are the most advanced Gulf states. Chapters 3 and 4 therefore focus on their respective development through the twentieth century, with special emphasis on current affairs.

One of the most outstanding features of the political evolution of the Gulf states has been the enduring and paramount role of the ruler. Chapter 5 analyses the functions of government today and sets the scene for Chapters 6, 7 and 8 which deal with the ruling dynasties of the five Gulf states.

Their external security is directly linked to Saudi Arabia. Chapter 9 presents the evolution of the changing phases of the Saudi relationship with the Gulf states. Finally, the impact of the Iraq–Iran war on the Gulf states is presented in Chapter 10.

1 The Gulf in History

The Land of Paradise

The Gulf region is one of the oldest continuously inhabited places in the world. According to ancient tradition, a fish-man, Oannes, swam up the Gulf, bringing with him the gifts of civilization. Five thousand years ago, its western coast was the centre of a flourishing civilization: that of the idyllic land of Dilmun whose landmarks are still in the process of being discovered. It was sacred to the Sumerians who venerated it in their poetry, referring to it alternatively as the Land of Paradise, the Land of the Living, and the Home of the Gods. It has been suggested that it was to Dilmun that the hero-king of the great *Epic of Gilgamesh* travelled in search of the survivor of the Universal Deluge; for Dilmun was the home of the god Ea, the friend of man.

Dilmun covered most of eastern Arabia and present-day Bahrain. It was a fertile and arable land with abundant water supplies; its irrigation and other agricultural activities were amongst the earliest to be known. It was not only a great religious and cultural centre, but also an important trading nation. Then, as today, its strategic location was one of its greatest assets: it lay between the great civilization of Sumer to the north and the Indus Valley to the east, taking in the ancient centre of Magan (Oman today) to the south. During the third and second millennia, the merchants of Dilmun carried a wide variety of goods between the east and the Mesopotamian city-states.

Dilmun was closely linked with Sumer, but it was not a dependency. Besides being a significant entrepôt, it produced two principal exports with which the Gulf region has been associated ever since: dates, the fruit of the palm trees which grow there in abundance; and the beautiful, luminous pearls of the Gulf waters, the 'fish-eyes' of the ancient texts.

Since those days, the destiny of the Gulf states has been linked with the centres of world power. Recent evidence has suggested, moreover, that the Gulf was the original homeland of the Phoenicians; their links with Egypt and Persia, the great powers of the day, obviously continued a well-established tradition.

But not only the Arab side of the Gulf was active. The Persian or eastern coast came into its own during the sixth century BC when the first Persian Empire was founded by Cyrus the Great. From that time to the present, political events in the Gulf have been punctuated by rivalry between the eastern and western coasts, between the Persians and the Arabs. Over this long period of time, a considerable intermingling of the two peoples has taken place. The Persians have lived on the Arab side to partake of the rich trade going on there, to escape political or commercial exploitation at home, or as a result of conquest, and the Arabs have lived on the Persian side for similar reasons. The result today is that the coastal populations of both sides of the Gulf contain a mixture of Arabs and Persians.

Alexander the Great had ambitions to build an empire in western Asia, and to this end he dispatched his admiral, Androsthenes of Thasos, to survey the Gulf region. The early death of Alexander, however, put an end to these plans. They were revived during the Roman period when the Emperor Augustus assigned Gaius Caesar, his adopted son and heir, to mount a campaign in Arabia: a number of 'strategic studies' were prepared for this. But during the periods of the Greek and Roman empires, the focii of their respective policies were in Europe, Africa and the eastern Mediterranean. Thus the Gulf region did not assume the same strategic importance it had enjoyed during the Babylonian period. This importance was revived in the seventh century AD with the birth of Islam. The Arabs were then propelled to international prominence.

The Arabian Nights

In the eighth century AD, Baghdad became the capital of the Abbasid caliphate. The Arab side of the Gulf once again became a major entrepôt for goods; it was also an important communications, strategic and financial centre. The court of Baghdad was a luxurious one, and the merchants of the Gulf provided it with a wide variety of goods: textiles and spices from India; porcelain, drugs and textiles from China. The exquisite pearls of the Gulf, amongst the most perfect in the world, were very much in demand at this time, for this was the era of *The Arabian Nights*, and of Caliph Haroun al-Rashid. The pearling industry, which had evolved over the centuries, became highly sophisticated and reflected the scientific and technological inclinations of the period. Detailed maps of the pearling banks were drawn up; so too were astonishingly thorough lists of the varieties of pearls available, including their shapes, weights and prices.

Trade at this time depended on the skills of the Arab navigators whose sailing ships regularly travelled the 6,000-mile journey to China. The story of Sindbad the Sailor in *The Arabian Nights* was based on their experiences. To re-create the extraordinary story of those early Arab sailors, Tim Severin undertook an epic voyage in 1980. He constructed a ship in the old way – using timber held together with coconut rope – and with a crew which included Omani sailors, he followed Sindbad's route from Oman to China. His experiences were recorded in his fascinating book, *The Sindbad Voyage* (London, 1982).

One of the thriving commercial centres of the Gulf during the early Abbasid period was Sohar in Oman. It is said to have been a very beautiful city whose population was made up of both Persians and Arabs. Less important, but active none the less, was Muscat. Once Baghdad became established as the capital of the Abbasid Caliphate, several commercial centres sprang up in the north of the Gulf; of these, Basra was perhaps the most notable. But the political upheavals caused both by the Zanj (slave) revolution which began there in 868, followed by the rebellion of the Qarmatians, with headquarters in the Bahrain islands, brought with them a serious disruption of trade. Alternative locations for the lucrative import–export activities were found on the Persian side of the Gulf from the early eleventh century onwards.

Siraf was the first of the major trading centres to evolve on the eastern coast. Its people, Arabs and Persians, continued the tradition of sailing to and from India and China. Siraf was succeeded in commercial importance by the island of Kishm, just over 60 kilometres (100 miles) away. Its population was predominantly Arab, as were its rulers. The next and possibly the most impressive of the trading emporia in the Gulf was the island of Hormuz which attained its apogee militarily and commercially from the early fourteenth century until the advent of the Portuguese.

The authority of Hormuz extended to several places on the Arab and Persian coasts, including the Bahrain islands whose pearls provided one of the main sources of Hormuz's income. But it was its strategic position at the mouth of the Gulf which was its most important characteristic, for otherwise it lacked water and had very little vegetation. Its place in the history of the Gulf is memorable. It was remarkably rich, with a large and varied population whose nucleus was, once again. Arabs and Persians. Its traders carried merchandise east and west, and its prosperity was manifestly obvious to all travellers who arrived there.

The beginnings of European colonialism

The prosperity of Hormuz, however, went into decline with the entry to Gulf waters of the Portuguese. It was the successful circumnavigation by Vasco da Gama of the Cape of Good Hope during the late fifteenth century which ushered in the era of European penetration. For subsequently the Portuguese made their push to the east, and the Gulf became coveted by foreign powers because of its strategic position on the rich route to India.

For the next four centuries, the Gulf became inextricably linked with the commercial and political rivalries of western countries: Portugal first, then Holland and France, and finally Britain. To this was added the rivalry of the Ottoman Empire; from the early sixteenth century when Baghdad and then Basra became a part of the Empire, the Gulf became an added concern of the Porte.

Portuguese domination of the Gulf reached its zenith during the sixteenth century. Albuquerque first took Muscat, thereby controlling most of the ports on the southern and eastern coasts of Oman; then Hormuz was captured in 1514, ushering in the decline of that great centre. Bahrain was added to the Portuguese possessions less than a decade later. Before long, the Portuguese were in full command of the great spice and silk route to India.

With time, however, two forces were to threaten Portugal's position severely and ultimately cause its withdrawal from the region. The first was that of the Ottomans, who had already defeated the Portuguese at Jeddah in 1517, thereby curbing their expansion in the Red Sea. The Ottomans then tried, unsuccessfully, to dislodge the Portuguese from Hormuz. The second force was that of Shah Abbas, the great Safavid ruler of Persia, whose rise to power was concurrent with his ambition to dominate Gulf waters. His first victory was in 1602 when he overran Bahrain; and then his final objective, to take back Hormuz, was brought about with the help of the English East India Company with which he had made an alliance.

It was not long before the Dutch and French East India Companies became involved in the region in an effort to offset the new foothold gained by the English. The whole of the seventeenth century was dominated by intense rivalry between the representatives of these three European companies.

In the meantime, both Arabs and Persians were gradually re-adjusting to their international environment. The arrival of the Portuguese had been a new experience for the region: for the first time, an outside power had held sway there. Although foreign powers were to retain their position in the region for close to 500 years, they had to struggle against opposition from local forces anxious to regain some of the lost territories.

The focus was Bahrain and Muscat, the two most important places on the Arab coast. Local powers began to contest European possession of them towards the middle of the seventeenth century. The first major battle occurred in 1660 when Muscat was regained from the Portuguese by the Yaaribah tribe of Oman; a few decades later, the same tribe successfully dislodged the Persians from Bahrain. But they were not to hold Bahrain for very long. For when Nadir Shah came to power in 1736, he was determined to extend his rule to both shores of the Gulf, like other strong rulers of Persia before and after him. To this end he built a navy and in 1753 he wrested control first of Bahrain and later of Muscat. The Persians, however, did not rule Muscat for long: they were finally expelled by the military forces of the (Arab) Governor of Sohar, Ahmad bin Said, the founder of the Al bu Said dynasty which rules Oman today. The Al bu Said consolidated their rule and regained for Oman its former position as a great trading centre. By the nineteenth century it had become a maritime empire under one of its greatest rulers, Said bin Sultan Al bu Said (1807–56).

The eighteenth-century framework

Almost concurrently with the establishment of the Al bu Said in Oman during the mid-eighteenth century, two major events occurred which were to have a lasting influence on the Gulf states.

The first of these was Clive's victories in India which established British dominance on the north-eastern coast of India, thus paving the way for further penetration of the sub-continent: this was to lead to the growth of British interests in the Gulf as a means of protecting its trade route to India.

The second event was the rise in central Arabia of the Wahhabi movement (named after its founder, Shaikh Muhammad ibn Abdel Wahhab), which was later to expand throughout the Arabian peninsula. Its basic ideology was to effect a return to the original principles of Islam; its main theological tenet was the oneness or unity of God. The Wahhabis forged an alliance early on with the Al Saud who ruled Dariyyah in Nejd (central Arabia). This alliance has been maintained and remains the basis of the Kingdom of Saudi Arabia today.

The ultimate emergence of British interests in the Gulf and the birth of the Wahhabi–Saudi movement together provided the framework for the modern Gulf region. Within this broadly based framework, a large number of processes occurred over the next 200 years which were to shape the Gulf states as we know them today.

One such process was the rise of the Qasimi (plural Qawasim) tribal confederacy which was achieving fame and notoriety well beyond the confines of Gulf waters. Their headquarters alternated over the years between Sharjah and Ras al-Khaimah (in the UAE today), and their power extended to both the Persian and Arab coasts. They commanded a remarkably large fleet, equipped for trade as well as warfare. It was said to have had around 900 vessels, many of which were swifter than European ships, and its naval force consisted of about 8,000 fighting men.

The appellation of 'pirates', which was given to the Qawasim by the Europeans from the seventeenth century on, has caused considerable controversy in recent times. Only in the past three or four decades have the citizens of the UAE become fully acquainted with the image projected of them in the past as sea-faring bandits; and they have since attempted to correct what they consider to be a misrepresentation of fact. The present Amir of Sharjah, Sultan Muhammad Al Qasimi, has researched the available records of the period; the results of his work have gone a long way to refuting the old image of the Qawasim, of which he is a member. His work was undertaken originally in the form of a Ph.D. dissertation at the University of Exeter, and was published in a recent book entitled *The Myth of Arab Piracy in the Gulf* (London, 1986).

The term is, of course, relative, and seems to have been used by English and Dutch traders who were angered when the Qawasim established a trading station on the island of Kishm off the Persian coast in the eighteenth century. The English East India Company had a major trading interest at the neighbouring station of Bandar Abbas and therefore stood to lose a fair amount on its customs dues and the Qasimi station. In order to ensure British supremacy in the immediate vicinity, therefore, a British naval expedition attacked and raided Kishm. The reason given for the attack and the consequent seizure of goods and money was to redress the balance of the loss in customs dues. The war between the Qawasim and the British had started.

The power of the Qawasim grew, rather than abated, throughout the eighteenth century. Moreover, they became allied with the Wahhabis, whose first major expansion reached the eastern coast of the Arabian peninsula; thereafter, the Qawasim can be regarded as having become the naval extension of the Wahhabi movement. This included the obtaining of tribute for the safe passage of merchant vessels.

The death knell of the Qawasim was sounded in 1809 when the British launched an expeditionary force against their principal headquarters in Ras al-Khaimah. Ras al-Khaimah was briefly occupied and most of the Qasimi fleet, which was lying off the town, was destroyed. This act of violence so incensed the Qawasim that they retaliated, rallying the neighbouring shaikhs of Umm al-Qaiwain, Ajman, Abu Dhabi, Dubai and Bahrain to their cause.

The Trucial system

They were ultimately to discover that they were no match for British sea power. In 1820, after a devastating siege of Ras al-Khaimah by British forces which was followed by the destruction of the entire Qasimi fleet, the trucial system was set in motion. The Qawasim and the shaikhs of Ajman, Umm al-Qaiwain, Abu Dhabi, Dubai and Bahrain capitulated and signed separate agreements with the British government. Each was known as the General Treaty of Peace and in it each shaikh bound himself to abstain from 'piracy' on land and at sea. By the same token,

Britain made it clear that it had no territorial or political ambitions in the area and that it would not interfere in local affairs.

The General Treaty of Peace constituted the genesis of the Gulf states as separate political units; and of their shaikhs as independent rulers, for that is how they were reflected in their new relationship with Britain. The Gulf states had thereby entered into 'treaty relations' with Britain.

The extent of these separate political units – and consequently how far the authority of their rulers extended – was not considered until over 100 years later when the oil companies became interested in the region. In the meantime, British interest focused on coastal areas because of the sea route between Britain and India.

The 1820 treaty protected British vessels from attack, but it did not prevent warfare at sea between the coastal tribes, so in 1835, the chiefs of Abu Dhabi, Dubai, Sharjah and Ajman signed a one-year truce in which they undertook to report any aggression to the British authorities rather than retaliate themselves. The truce was renewed the next year and at various intervals until 1853 when the Perpetual Maritime Truce was signed and the shaikhs undertook to call a halt to all hostilities at sea.

The states whose rulers had signed the Perpetual Maritime Truce became known as Trucial states, a name which persisted until 1971 when they united to form the federation called the United Arab Emirates. Two main groupings have dominated the Trucial states: the Qawasim and the Bani Yas. The latter are a land power, different branches of which rule over Dubai and Abu Dhabi. Because seafaring had been the most important activity until the treaties with Britain, the Qawasim had been the dominant force on the coast.

One of the most significant repercussions of the new relationship with Britain was the gradual decline of the Qawasim, whose seafaring activities, the basis of their power, were curtailed, and the subsequent rise of the Bani Yas. By the end of the nineteenth century, the latter assumed a position of primary importance in the Trucial states. That position was maintained until the 1950s; Abu Dhabi commanded a large inland stretch of land and Dubai had evolved into an important trading centre. The position of the Bani Yas was reinforced by the coincidental discovery of vast oil reserves in Abu Dhabi in 1958, and the continued growth of Dubai's commercial importance. Abu Dhabi and Dubai are by far the most influential and crucial members of the UAE today.

Although its shaikh had signed the General Treaty of Peace in 1821, Bahrain did not become part of the trucial system until 1861. It then undertook to abstain from all forms of maritime hostilities; in exchange for this undertaking, Britain promised to protect it from attack by sea.

Treaty relations

Britain thus came to regard the region as its own preserve. But towards the end of the nineteenth century, its supremacy began to be challenged by other powers – the Ottoman Empire, France, Russia and Germany. British diplomacy spared no effort at this time to assert its omnipotence along two fronts. It diminished the position of its foreign rivals by drawing up an elaborate series of conventions and agreements with them; and at the same time it redefined and confirmed its special status with local rulers by another set of treaties, some of which were to remain in force until 1971.

Following fears of the establishment of an Ottoman presence in Bahrain, Britain secured an agreement from the shaikh in 1880. In it the ruler bound himself, his heirs and successors not to enter into negotiations of any kind with any power without the consent of the British government. He also undertook not to accept the establishment of any kind of foreign agency without British approval.

The climax of this type of agreement was reached in 1892 when Exclusive Agreements were signed by the rulers of the Trucial states and Bahrain. The former bound themselves, their heirs and successors to the same conditions as had the ruler of Bahrain in 1880. In addition, all rulers (of the Trucial states and Bahrain) signed a non-alienation bond with Britain; this meant that they could not cede, sell or lease any part of their territories to any power other than Britain.

After Ahmad bin Said liberated Muscat, he then went on to expel the Persians from all Omani territory in 1744 and establish the Al bu Said dynasty. His grandson, Said bin Sultan (1807–56), extended his authority to Zanzibar in east Africa. After his death, the fortunes of Oman declined considerably. One reason was the disputes between his two sons, who constituted a ruling duumvirate; one was based in Zanzibar, the other in Muscat. Britain became involved in the arbitration of the disputes between the brothers, and in 1861 was instrumental in severing Zanzibar from Oman. Oman became so impoverished by the truncation of its most important possession that it was forced over the years to rely entirely on a British subsidy: in return, Britain obtained much greater control over Omani affairs.

Kuwait and Qatar alone remained outside the British sphere of influence until 1899 and 1916 respectively. In both cases, their rulers were anxious to join the other Gulf states in the treaty system in order to escape Ottoman overlordship. The skilful manner in which both men were able to manage circumstances often beyond their control went a long way to promoting the establishment of their respective states as independent political units. In 1899, the ruler of Kuwait signed a non-alienation bond with Britain and undertook not to receive any foreign agent or representative without British sanction. In 1916, Qatar joined the system; its ruler signed an Exclusive Agreement similar to those of the Trucial states and Bahrain.

By the early twentieth century, then, Britain had obtained a position of dominance in the Gulf which was to last until 1971. Although at first its main interest in the region had been commercial, this was eventually supplanted by a policy whose objectives were purely political. Its early dealings with the rulers of the Gulf states had been undertaken by the British government of Bombay. After 1873, responsibility for Gulf affairs was transferred to the British government of India. The region was administered locally through a Political Resident who was stationed at Bushire in southern Iran until 1946, when his headquarters were moved to Bahrain. Subordinate to him were Political Agents who at different times were stationed in Kuwait, Bahrain, Sharjah and Muscat. After India became independent in 1947, the British government of India was dissolved. Thereafter, responsibility for Gulf affairs was assumed by the Foreign Office in London. The system of Political Resident and Agents remained in force until 1971 when treaty relations were terminated.

The last significant group of treaties with Britain concerned the awarding of oil concessions. These were signed between 1913 and 1922 by the different rulers who undertook not to award any oil concession except to a company appointed by the British government. 'Let it not be hidden from you that we agree, if oil is expected to be found in our territory, not to grant any concession in this connection to anyone except to the person appointed by

the High British Government.'[1] This was the undertaking signed
by the ruler of Dubai in 1922.

Note

1   C. U. Aitchison, *A Collection of Treaties, Engagements and Sanads
Relating to India and Neighbouring Countries*, fifth edition (Delhi,
1933), vol. 11, p. 261.

2 The Emergence of the Gulf States

Two major external factors have played a determining role in the establishment and evolution of the Gulf states: their strategic location on the route to India, which led directly to the relationship with Britain, and the existence there of vast oil resources, which has had far-reaching and inevitable economic and political repercussions. The interaction of these two has in turn had a significant effect on another important factor, the central authority of the ruler, whose position became institutionalized. This chapter will analyse the emergence of the modern Gulf states in the light of these three factors – strategy, oil and the position of the ruler – which can be said to have had the greatest bearing on their formation.

Strategy: relationship with Britain

British ships first went to the Gulf because of its position on the route to India; this led ultimately to the establishment of British dominance in the region. Throughout the nineteenth century, Britain had been concerned with promoting the access of its vessels sailing to and from India. To this end, it spun an intricate web of treaties around the Arab rulers of the Gulf states. By the end of World War I, the Gulf had become, to all intents and purposes, a British lake.

The strategic assets of the Gulf region increased even further during the twentieth century. In Iran oil was discovered and produced by a British company (the Anglo-Persian Oil Company, the predecessor of British Petroleum); in Iraq Britain had assumed a mandate; and important landing and refuelling stops were established for the British air route linking Egypt, Iraq and India (Kuwait, Bahrain, Sharjah, Oman).

Throughout the period of British hegemony, many of the

features which were to constitute important characteristics of the Gulf states were established. They owe much of their existence as separate political units to Britain. Their rulers were personally responsible for fulfilling their treaty conditions, and they alone had dealings with British officials and representatives. The fact of their treaty obligations gave the rulers continuity and political status, for they bound both them and their heirs and successors.

By and large, the treaties with Britain sealed the Gulf states off from the rest of the world. Britain guarded them with a jealous eye: in the nineteenth century, to prevent other powers from entering the region; and in the present century, to ensure the maintenance of the Gulf as a British lake. On the one hand, therefore, the British connection added an important element to the sovereignty of the states and their rulers; and on the other, that connection isolated the states, thus impeding their socio-political development.

This isolation caused the states over the years to become very parochial and inward-looking; until the discovery of oil, they appeared to be places where time had stood still. The merchants and sailors confined their activities to the shores of the Gulf, and ventured out only as far as Bombay. Until the recent past the Indian connection remained very strong. The Indian rupee was the currency in circulation, particularly in the coastal towns and villages, and until the 1940s, Indian stamps were overmarked 'Kuwait' and 'Bahrain'. The Arabic dialect of the coastal areas contained many Urdu words, and the political officers stationed there – a mere handful of Englishmen – were members of the British government of India who had been trained for service in India. They applied British Indian regulations throughout the Gulf states.

Most of the Gulf states had no recognized legal status within the British Empire. They were not colonies, mandates or protectorates; they were described simply as being 'in treaty relations with Britain'. The fact that they were a backwater, however, afforded them a certain protection, acting as a cocoon which preserved their social traditions and political systems, permitting the continued use of Arab tribal customs. It also contributed to the survival of their institutions despite the dramatic impact of the great oil wealth of the past forty years.

No Gulf state was allowed to deal directly with another country, large or small; all foreign relations were conducted on their behalf by Britain until independence. Moreover, all movement in and out of the Gulf states was subject to British permission. An amazing anecdote will illustrate this point. In 1934, the Political Agent in Bahrain received a telegram from the British consul in Basra informing him that he had granted an entry visa to Bahrain to a Mr Harding of American Express. The Agent panicked when he read the telegram; he did not want any Americans in Bahrain. He therefore decided to prevent Mr Harding's entry. He went to the airport and prepared to send him back immediately after his plane landed, but to his surprise and relief, Mr Harding turned out to be an Englishman; he was allowed in.

The net result of this tight control was that the people of the Gulf were cut off from the rest of the world except India. They had little to do with their fellow Arabs until the advent of oil, with the exception of a tiny group of Egyptian, Lebanese and Palestinian schoolteachers in Kuwait and Bahrain.

By the same token, the British relationship also acted to protect the political and territorial integrity of the different states. This was particularly the case during the 1920s and 1930s when the three regional powers – Saudi Arabia, Iran and Iraq – entered the political arena. The first two were dominated by charismatic personalities: King Abdel Aziz ibn Abdel Rahman Al Faisal Al Saud (known in the West as King Ibn Saud) and Reza Shah. After having consolidated their own power at home, both men gradually led their respective countries to become important components in the political structure of the region. After attaining independence from Britain in 1930, Iraq joined Saudi Arabia and Iran to become the third regional power.

All three laid claim to different parts of the Gulf states, and all three were engaged in a forward policy there during the inter-war years. The King of Saudi Arabia considered parts of the inland territories of Oman, Qatar and the Trucial states as belonging to his kingdom. Likewise, Reza Shah revived the old Iranian claim to Bahrain, and Iraq regarded Kuwait as part of the Ottoman province of Basra from which it had been separated by the Anglo-Kuwaiti treaty of 1899.

Britain resisted these claims with great firmness, and expended considerable diplomatic and political effort to maintain the *status quo*. As a result, the regional powers confined manifestations of these claims to non-military means. The forward policies of the regional powers were thereby contained and frozen into the requirements of the *pax Britannica*. These requirements were so firmly established that they have been maintained up to the present, albeit in a different form, long after Britain has left the region.

An interesting feature of the British connection before the discovery of oil was the smallness of the contingent of British officals residing there; until World War II, they were never more than four or five. They alone maintained British rule and made sure the treaty conditions were observed. They issued manumission certificates for slaves wishing to be released from their bondage. They had meetings with the rulers, and kept detailed records of all events of importance. They had jurisdiction over most foreigners in the Gulf states. On the commercial side, their functions included the issuing of certificates of origin for shipping, approving lists of passengers and granting export licences. Their authority was, of course, upheld at all times by the sloops of the British Indian navy, which were never far off; their stated objective was to secure and maintain the maritime peace of the Gulf.

British policy was officially against interference in the internal affairs of the states so long as British interests were not affected. The British officials living there were so few that their duties were very time-consuming. None of the modern amenities – such as electricity, air-conditioning, refrigerators – were then available, and daily life was fairly difficult for these Europeans who were not accustomed to the heat and humidity.

The policy of non-interference meant that British officials were not involved in the introduction of any of the much-needed socioeconomic reforms. No schools or hospitals, no public services of any kind were introduced by the representatives of the British government: this perpetuated the isolation of the region.

It also contributed to the strengthening of the respective positions of the different rulers. Government was left entirely to them so long as they fulfilled their treaty obligations; these were largely concerned with the absence both of foreign relations and of any kind of hostilities at sea. The rulers received moral and political support from Britain, and were allowed a free hand in the conduct of local affairs. They therefore gained much in stature during the British period.

The fact that Britain had separate relations with all the states, large or small, encouraged feelings of separation between them. A clause in the treaties stipulated, for example, that every ship had to fly the flag of the state to which it belonged. In time, each state became identified with a flag. The daily identification with its own flag by each seafaring population increased the separateness, and played a part in establishing the difference between, say, Dubai and Sharjah, and between Qatar and Abu Dhabi.

Travel documents were issued by British officials. Although a flag and a passport are only symbols of a state, their repeated use inevitably brings about a form of national identity. The natural corollary to a flag and a passport is a national anthem. Although it is unlikely that any of the Gulf states had anthems in the modern sense during the nineteenth century, Bahrain and Oman had such a song by the 1930s, and today all Gulf states have them.

Flags, passports and anthems are only very minor manifestations of separateness, but in the Gulf they contributed, over the many years of the British presence, to the process by which each state became politically and socially self-contained. In the same way, the parcelling off of small groups of tribal configurations to become separate political units led to other, perhaps more lasting, results, the most outstanding of which concerns oil. Since the British government of India oversaw all the original oil concessions, it was only natural for it to introduce the oil companies to the same political units. Thus, the signing of the oil concessions perpetuated the political system created in the nineteenth century: separate concessions were granted to the oil companies by the rulers of Qatar and Umm al-Qaiwain, Dubai and Abu Dhabi. Since oil was not discovered in all the Gulf states, Kuwait, Abu Dhabi and Qatar are today particularly rich, while Fujairah, Bahrain and Umm al-Qaiwain are not.

Oil: the advent of the companies

The entry of the oil companies in search of concessions soon after World War I was to become a major milestone in the sociopolitical and economic evolution of the region. Their influence was felt in two different areas simultaneously. On the one hand, they upheld and perpetuated the political units which had evolved and developed under British aegis; on the other, they acted as agents of major change. The two effects were mutually reinforcing. The impact of the oil companies was so strong that it has allowed the Gulf states to maintain their old political systems long after the end of the colonial era.

Since the oil companies worked very closely with British officials, it was inevitable that they too would regard each state as separate. A concession with specific terms and conditions for Bahrain was signed with the ruler in 1930; another one with Kuwait was signed in 1934; the ruler of Qatar signed his in 1935; and so on. The concessions ultimately determined the course of the financial fortunes of each state: Kuwait became and has remained enormously wealthy since 1949–50; Bahrain only moderately so in the 1930s; and Ras al-Khaimah and Sharjah have started only recently to reap the financial rewards of the discovery of oil. By placing the concessions in the names of the different rulers, the oil companies helped to maintain the political system.

They also raised a new question when dealing with the political units. This was one with which the British authorities had not been hitherto concerned – the precise delineation of each state's boundaries. The companies understandably wanted to know the exact extent of their concessionary areas and turned to the British officials for information. Every inch of land had suddenly become very valuable.

The Gulf states had never before attempted to define their borders. The desert law that governed society was not concerned with such a foreign concept. Qatar, the Trucial states and Oman all had large inland territories; their boundaries fluctuated according to pastoral and political conditions, and were never expected to achieve any degree of permanence. Rupert Hay, who was Political Resident during the 1950s, described the situation as follows: 'The Arabian desert has sometimes been compared to the high seas. Caravans come and go like ships and nomads roam at will in search of grazing . . .'[1]

The very acceptance of the principle of boundaries at this time served to underline the separateness of each state and thus to cause each to identify itself as a separate political unit. It was inevitable that tension – and, in some cases, hostilities – between neighbouring states resulted: each extended its territorial claim to the largest possible area.

Kuwait's borders had already been delineated in 1922 at a conference held under British auspices in Ujair (Saudi Arabia) to limit the expansion of Saudi Arabia into Iraq; two-thirds of the land claimed by Kuwait at that time was 'awarded' to Saudi Arabia by the British authorities. In addition, those areas whose sovereignty could not be accurately defined were designated 'neutral zones': they were to be shared equally by the two states.

The difficult task of defining borders and determining the exact extent of a ruler's authority began in earnest after the preliminary concessions were signed during the 1930s. Hitherto, a ruler's sovereignty had been firmly established only in the coastal towns, and occasionally in the inland oases such as al-Ain and Liwa (Abu Dhabi). This was because Britain, primarily interested in the sea route to India, recognized the authority only of those rulers who had jurisdiction over coastal areas.

Bahrain's island status presented no problems and Kuwait's borders had been established in 1922. The inland portions of the remainder of the states included large tracts of desert. The seeds of the first major dispute over territory were sown when Saudi Arabia granted an oil concession in 1933 to an American oil company. The Foreign Office in London, acting on behalf of Oman, Qatar and Abu Dhabi – whose borders were contiguous with Saudi Arabia – defined their exact extent shortly afterwards. This was rejected by Saudi Arabia, and thus began a major territorial dispute between Saudi Arabia on the one hand and the three Gulf states on the other which was to affect relations between them for the next four decades.

Territorial disputes between most of the Gulf states ensued within a few years of the signing of the preliminary oil concessions: between Qatar and Bahrain over Zubarah (on the west coast of Qatar) and the Hawar islands lying between them; between Abu Dhabi and Dubai; between Abu Dhabi and Qatar; between Sharjah and Dubai; and so on. Many of these have lingered on to the present day. The conflict which erupted in April 1986 between Qatar and Bahrain over the islet of Fasht al-Dibal (belonging to the Hawar islands) is the continuation of a problem which started when the oil concessions were signed in the 1930s.

One of the most striking changes brought about by the oil companies was the opening up of the region to the outside world. Until then, the British authorities had granted very few entry visas there, and allowed only minimal reference to the Gulf states to be made internationally. Once the oil concessions had been signed, control of foreigners could no longer be tightly restricted; geologists, refinery workers, managers, etc. all began to arrive in increasing numbers. The parochial days of the Gulf states were over.

As the barriers of isolation were lifted, an awareness of the political and economic realities of the Gulf region began to grow. From hesitant beginnings, Egyptian, Syrian and Iraqi newspapers, which began to arrive there on a regular basis, turned their attention to the eastern flank of the Arab world. Relationships with Arab countries were gradually established. At first, they were confined mostly to the cultural level as Gulf students began to go abroad: Bahrainis to Lebanon, Kuwaitis to Egypt and Iraq. Moreover, Egyptian, Palestinian and Lebanese teachers arrived in Kuwait and Bahrain. Gulf citizens, particularly those of the privileged élite, felt stronger bonds with their fellow Arabs than they had had with Indians. The earlier links with India soon assumed second place.

Another new link was also being forged: that with the USA, whose interests in the Gulf and the entire Arab world had hitherto been confined largely to the activities of a few missionaries. It was in Bahrain that an American oil company, the Standard Oil Company of California (SoCal), first obtained a concession. Although the British government had initially objected strongly to the entry of a US company, it finally accepted it on condition that the company holding the Bahrain concession would be a British company. So a subsidiary of SoCal, the Bahrain Petroleum Company (BAPCO) was formed as a British company which was registered in Canada; one of its five directors was British and his appointment was always made in consultation with the British government. BAPCO struck oil in Bahrain in 1931, and production began the following year. In 1933, SoCal obtained a concession for Saudi Arabia. American oil companies were now firmly established in the region, their interests ultimately providing the basis for a forward US policy in the Arab world. A new power was set to overtake Britain.

The position of ruler

The combined effect of the relationship with Britain and the opening of the region by the oil companies had a powerful local impact on the role of central authority. The one important and constant element in the political evolution of the Gulf states was the position of the ruler. He signed the treaties, and he was personally responsible for the application of all their clauses. The British authorities – whether the Political Resident, the Political Agent or the Senior Naval Officer of the Persian Gulf Division – dealt with him alone. The treaty system strengthened his position and assured the continuity of his influence. With time, it became

a guarantee. Most important, it contributed to the institutionalization of his position.

British support for a ruler was conveyed in many different ways,
even in the number of gun salutes he was accorded. In 1929,
for example, the rulers of Kuwait, Bahrain and Qatar were the
recipients of seven-gun salutes; the ruler of Abu Dhabi received
a five-gun salute; and the ruler of Dubai, only a humble three.
That year, an attempt was made by the family of Shaikh Said of
Dubai to depose him. The Political Resident stepped in to uphold
the ruler: he warned that any move to depose Shaikh Said would
incur the strong disapproval of the British government. To re-
confirm this support, a public and audible gesture to Shaikh Said
followed: he was granted a five-gun salute. This was a clear recognition of his independence and one that reflected his increased
stature.

By the same token, the salute for Abu Dhabi was reduced
because of fratricide in the ruling family: between 1912 and 1928,
three rulers were murdered by their brothers who then succeeded
them. The gun salute was reduced from five to three as a symbol
of British displeasure. Likewise, the salutes of Kuwait and Bahrain
were raised (to eleven) as a mark of approbation after they signed
oil concessions a few years later.

Before the arrival of the oil companies, the rulers had assumed
a generally passive role in their respective relationships with
Britain. As long as they adhered to their treaty conditions, they
had little contact with British officials, aside from formalities. But
once negotiations for oil concessions had started, the situation
changed perceptibly. The ruler now became more active and
dynamic; his signature was essential to the business in hand, and
he was allowed to participate in the discussions, which had become
tri-lateral: those taking part were the Political Agent, a representative of the oil company and the ruler. The ruler was quick to
perceive that he had new advantages, and acted on this with
positive results.

He was aware of the economic benefits – though not perhaps
of their extent – that could be derived from the discovery of oil.
He therefore held out for the best financial terms possible. Shaikh
Ahmad al-Jabir of Kuwait went one step further. He encouraged
two different companies, the Gulf Oil Corporation (USA) and
the Anglo-Iranian Oil Company (Britain) to outbid each other
while competing for the same concession. He therefore obtained

better terms; he astutely waited for the opportune moment, and awarded it to both companies on a fifty-fifty basis.

A ruler could also opt for political rather than commercial gains during the tri-lateral discussions for an oil concession. Such was the case of Shaikh Abdallah of Qatar in 1935. Since the early days of his rule, he had been plagued by the hostility of his brothers, over whom he had little control. He required a firm British commitment both to safeguard his position and to recognize his son as his heir and successor. He therefore struck a bargain with the Political Resident: he would sign the oil concession if Britain provided him with such a commitment. His position as ruler was thereby strengthened considerably.

A ruler was personally responsible to Britain for the actions of his people. Any infringement of the treaty regulations could bring British admonition down on him. His successor would emerge from his immediate family. The law of primogeniture did not apply in the Gulf: the main principle governing the succession was the strength and abilities of the candidate. He had to display a combination of fearlessness, integrity, intelligence, wisdom and generosity; he also had to make sure that none of his close relatives became disaffected – not to do so could bring about his downfall. The most important factor in his selection was his qualities of leadership. He could be the son of the ruler, the brother, the nephew or the uncle. This fact inevitably led to great rivalries and tensions within the ruling families, as the members vied with each other for control.

With the exception of the Al Khalifah, who had come to power in Bahrain as a result of conquest, the ruling families had emerged over the years through the efforts of individuals with outstanding leadership abilities. A close rapport with their citizens evolved by the twentieth century with the institutionalization of their respective positions.

The British policy of non-interference allowed the rulers a relatively free hand in governing. Although in principle they had absolute power, they generally consulted a small, informal council (*majlis*) according to the Islamic principle of *shura* (consultation). The concept of *shura* was essential to the administration of authority. Most decisions of importance were obtained in that manner: they were referred to the *majlis*, which usually contained one or two members of the ruling family, together with social and religious notables.

This system of shared responsibility prompted Bertram Thomas, who was Financial Adviser to the Sultan of Muscat, to remark that it had 'its own kind of democracy, namely, a social democracy side by side with traditional authoritarianism in government (largely this is the converse of British democracy)'.[2] If a ruler failed to consult his *majlis*, he could expect the notables to band together to oblige him to do so.

The administrative infrastructure was very limited, and the functions of government varied from place to place. But the rulers remained accessible to their people: they gave daily audiences of several hours; they heard petitions and acted on them; they also gave judgments on personal and commercial disputes.

The economic activities of the states provided the rulers and their dependents with their main sources of income: in Oman, this was agriculture; in the other places, it was trade and the pearling industry. Other sources of income included customs dues and taxes on seafaring vessels. The extent of a ruler's income was directly related to his power and standing in the community; this affected the rhythm of economic activity and determined whether taxes could be imposed and collected. A state of economic interdependence existed between the ruler and his people.

The pearling industry was vital to the pre-oil economies. The work of pearling was extremely arduous, and sophisticated methods for its development had emerged over the centuries of exploiting the oyster-rich waters of the Gulf. The employment provided by the pearling industry gives a strong indication of its central role in society. In Kuwait, for example, 20 per cent of the entire population were engaged in it; in the Trucial states the figure was 31 per cent; and in Qatar 48 per cent.

The pearling industry suffered an almost total collapse after the Wall Street crash of 1929. The world economic depression which followed drastically lowered the demand for costly luxury items, such as pearls. The industry received another blow when the Japanese introduced cultured pearls into the international market shortly afterwards. During the 1930s, therefore, the economy of the Gulf was shattered. It would have been almost impossible to overcome this crisis had the strange hand of fate not intervened: the oil companies arrived in search of concessions.

The oil concessions not only offered the possibility of relief from the poverty which had set in after 1929. They also brought about a subtle and important change in the relationship between a ruler and his people. The agreements provided the rulers with monthly retainer fees. Infinitesimal though these payments were, they allowed the rulers for the first time to be financially independent of their people. On the one hand, therefore, this drove a new and unexpected wedge between ruler and ruled; on the other, it allowed the rulers to become generous to their people without taxation.

When oil was discovered, the tiny trickle of money became a giant waterfall. Once again, the same situation prevailed. The ruler became the major recipient of the income; at the same time, he disbursed large sums of it towards socio-economic development projects. Before long, the Gulf states had become welfare states.

But the old system was considerably weakened. Once the oil revenues started to pour in, the former rudimentary methods of ruling were inevitably out of date. Complex government machinery was brought in: departments were set up, councils of ministers were appointed, secretaries and under-secretaries were employed, salary scales were drawn up.

This machinery contributed even more to widening the gap between the ruler and his people. The direct nature of the ruler's daily audiences became diffused, and access to him much more difficult. Previously, his citizens could approach him about any outstanding problems, no matter how personal. Now their requests and petitions had to be channelled through an ever-burgeoning bureaucracy. Although the old forum had not been dispensed with, a new system was superimposed upon it. The interdependence between ruler and ruled was broken. The search for a new form of participation began, and it was most marked in Kuwait and Bahrain. The following two chapters will survey their attempts.

Notes

1 Sir Rupert Hay, 'The Persian Gulf States and their Boundary Disputes', *Geographical Journal*, vol. 120, 1954, p. 435.
2 India Office Records, London. L/P&S/12/4584: Ext. 6051/42: Bertram Thomas (Public Relations Officer in the Persian Gulf) to S. F. Newcombe (Ministry of Information), 16 October 1942. Unpublished Crown Copyright material in the India Office Records and Public Record Office transcribed here appear by permission of the Controller of Her Majesty's Stationery Office.

3 Representative Government in Kuwait

The Year of the Majlis

In early May 1985, the National Assembly of Kuwait which was the only elected parliament in the Gulf, enforced the resignation of Shaikh Salman al-Duaij Al Sabah, the Minister of Justice. He had been accused of using his position as a cabinet minister and a member of the ruling family for personal gain. He admitted that he had obtained around $7 million for his twelve-year-old son from a special government fund which had been set up to compensate small investors after the collapse ofthe unofficial stock market known as the Suq al-Manakh. The National Assembly had also questioned the policies of Shaikh Ali Khalifah Al Sabah, the Minister for Oil and Industry. Allegations were made that he had used his office to provide inside information on government purchases to investors. Although there was a certain amount of pressure on him to resign, it might have had grave results had a second member of the ruling family, the Al (family of) Sabah, been hounded out of his position by the Assembly. The balance between the Al Sabah and the Assembly was maintained.

In the course of Kuwait's history, popular participation in government has frequently taken place on an informal level. But it was not until 1918 that a group of notables joined together and decided that a formal *majlis*, or advisory council, should be established as an officially recognized means of checking the ruler's powers and protecting the rights of the people. The notables approached the Political Agent, who was sympathetic to their proposal. Although the idea was not immediately taken up, it did not lie dormant for long.

It was revived in 1920 when Kuwait was undergoing a period of great insecurity. Wahhabi forces were attacking Kuwaiti caravans and raiding tribes under Kuwaiti protection. (It was at this time that a new fortifying wall around Kuwait town was built.) In one of their raids, the Wahhabis succeeded in besieging the Kuwaitis at a fort in Jahra, a few miles from Kuwait town. The battle of Jahra which followed is known to every Kuwaiti school-child; for the Kuwaitis fought courageously and succeeded in holding back the enemy. The outcome is also important. For once again the notables grouped together and impressed upon the ruler the urgent necessity of calling on Britain for help. The ruler agreed, and Britain responded by sending aeroplanes, sloops of war and armoured cars which so alarmed the Wahhabis that they withdrew.

The notables who had grouped together in an unofficial *majlis* (assembly), thereby saving the day, were the merchants who were feeling alienated from the Al Sabah. The families of most of these merchants had settled Kuwait in the early eighteenth century along with the Al Sabah. Like the latter, they were members of the Anaiza tribe of Nejd. These were: the Al Ghanim, who today own some of the biggest enterprises of Kuwait; the Al Saqr whose senior member, Abdel Aziz, is chairman of the Kuwait Chamber of Commerce; the Al Badr; the Al Shimlan; and the Al Qatami, a member of which has been a leading figure of the opposition and of the National Assembly. Another group of wealthy merchants had their origins in Zubair, in southern Iraq today. These are the Al Bahr and the Al Hamad, one of whose members is Abdel Latif Al Hamad, the present Director General of the Arab Fund for Economic and Social Development, and former Minister of Finance.

Over the years, a special relationship had developed between the ruling family and the leading merchant families. It took the form of an unofficial agreement between the two. The Al Sabah exerted their skill, power and influence so that Kuwait might remain secure and independent, and their dynasty retain command; the merchants, who were thus allowed to pursue their business activities, acknowledged the leadership of the Al Sabah and made voluntary financial contributions to them from the profits they enjoyed under the Al Sabah's protection.

During this process, however, the merchants become pros-perous in contrast to the Al Sabah, whose other duties prevented them from joining the business community in its commercial pursuits. But from the mid-nineteenth century on, the situation

began to change as Kuwait moved closer to the Ottoman administration in Iraq. Commercial links with Basra were strengthened
by military alliances, and during the same period, the Al Sabah
were acquiring substantial date groves in the Fao area; by the end
of the nineteenth century, these were to provide them with their
main private income. The Al Sabah thus possessed a new and
independent source of income. The ties which had bound the
merchant notables to the Al Sabah were beginning to loosen.

They continued to do so during the reign of Muhammad bin
Sabah (1892–6), who strengthened Kuwait's links with the Ottoman–Iraqi administration; this aroused the apprehension of many
of the notables, who feared the incorporation of Kuwait into the
Ottoman Empire. The policies of Muhammad's successor, his
brother Mubarak the Great (1896–1915), did little to restore the
old relationship with the merchants. He was a very forceful ruler
and is today regarded as the founder of the modern state of
Kuwait. It was during his reign that Kuwait first entered into
treaty relations with Britain. His position and prestige grew
immeasurably as a result of this new relationship. To enable him
to carry out his ambitious plans, he levied increasingly heavy
taxes. Relations between the merchants and the ruler were so
badly strained during his reign that a number of the former
became disheartened and left the country to settle in neighbouring
Bahrain. Although Mubarak, who was aware of the importance
of the merchants, was able to persuade them to return home, the
rift between the two groups had become a feature of Kuwaiti
political life.

The rift was formalized in 1921, after the death of Salim al-
Mubarak (1917–21) and just before his successor came to power.
The merchants presented the Al Sabah with their conditions for
the acceptance of the new ruler. According to the Kuwaiti author,
Salem al-Jabir Al Sabah (son of the present Amir), in *Les Emirats
du Golfe: Histoire d'un Peuple*,[1] their demands took the form of
a written charter. The fifth and last clause of the charter asked
for the election of a fixed number of people both from the Al
Sabah and the citizens of Kuwait to direct national affairs on
principles of justice and equality.

The most prominent candidate for the succession, Shaikh
Ahmad al-Jabir (1921–50), accepted these conditions before
becoming ruler. He committed himself further at the time and
promised to abide by the final decisions of the *ulama* (religious

leaders) in any disputed legal cases. Above all, he promised to consult his people in all matters and to consider any proposal put forward for the betterment of Kuwait town. An advisory council made up of twelve leading men was duly formed.

It was not to be active, however. Despite his promises, Shaikh Ahmad ignored the council and ruled in much the same manner as his immediate predecessors. In the meantime, more pressing problems confronted Kuwait, thereby diverting the attention of the rather resentful council members. The 1920s and 1930s were marked by great economic hardship which affected most Kuwaitis, leading merchants and pearl divers alike. There were two main reasons for this: first, a Saudi economic blockade of Kuwait which stifled its thriving entrepôt trade; second, the collapse of the pearling industry which all but put an end to the single most important source of Kuwait's livelihood.

In times of economic stress, political activity inevitably increases. Once again, it centred on the merchant notables, who came together to discuss their economic future. Politics became an important theme. Moreover, as a result of the activities of the Kuwait Oil Company after the preliminary concession was signed in 1934, the ties of British control were loosened, and for the first time, the people of Kuwait became actively aware of events in the Arab world.

This awareness was stimulated by the media, the newspapers and the radio. Kuwait's closest ties were with Iraq, largely because of geographical proximity. Many of the well-to-do sent their sons there to study; some owned property in the area around Basra; and some even held Iraqi nationality. It was around this time that an Association of Gulf Arabs was formed in Basra to promote the unity of Kuwait and Iraq.

In response to the general strike in Palestine and the subsequent civil disturbances there from 1936 to 1939, the strong feelings of Arab nationalism which swept through Iraq under the leadership of King Ghazi also found echoes in Kuwait. The ruler, Shaikh Ahmad al-Jabir, was very cautious in evincing support for the Palestinians, since he was constrained by his treaty relations with Britain. The Political Agent cautioned him against becoming involved in the Palestine problem because of its strong anti-British overtones and because of the feelings of Arab nationalism it evoked. The ruler therefore forbade any public contributions to be made.

This incurred the anger of the merchants, who defied his orders: generous contributions were made despite the unfavourable financial situation. After the contents of the Peel Commission Report recommending the partition of Palestine were made public in 1937, twelve leading Kuwaiti merchants formed a committee to protest to the British government. Once again, the ruler did not lend his support, and forbade his cousin, Shaikh Abdallah al-Salim, to preside over another committee which had been formed to collect money for Palestine.

The events in Palestine polarized the opposition to the ruler. The members of the different committees which had been established to collect money and make political protests were the leading merchants. Their defiance of the ruler's orders revived the memory of the broken agreement of 1921, and strengthened their ties with one another; in doing so, it crystallized their quest for political reform and economic development. They continued in opposition to the ruler as the Palestine problem grew in intensity and as their local grievances remained unresolved. Moreover, the ruler had recently (1934) signed a preliminary oil concession according to which he received a regular income. The generation of this income was, of course, totally independent of his people. This compounded the imbalance in the political structure.

The group of merchants who had been active politically became the nucleus of the opposition movement. Its strength continued to grow until it prevailed on the ruler to recognize the establishment of the National Legislative Council (*Majlis al-umma al-tashrii'i*) to carry out reforms and undertake economic development. The Council was presided over by the ruler's cousin, Shaikh Abdallah al-Salim, and consisted of fourteen members, who were elected on 29 June 1938.

The law governing the powers of the Majlis was signed by the ruler ten days later, authorizing it to oversee the budget, justice, public security, education, urban improvement and emergencies. The Majlis was also given the right to ratify all treaties and concessions signed by the ruler. Abdallah al-Salim was named the chief executive power in the land. The Majlis therefore was legislative and executive, as well as having some degree of judicial power. The power and authority of the ruler were much diminished.

Although the fourteen members of the Majlis were elected, voting and candidacy were restricted to the 150 leading families.

The members of that first Majlis belonged to families still prominent today. They included: Khalid Abdel Latif Al Hamad; Sulayman Khalid Al Adsani; Abdel Latif Muhammad Thunayyan Al Ghanim; Abdallah Hamad Al Saqr; Mishari Hasan Al Badr. Their families had been much wealthier in the nineteenth century when they also had more political power. The Majlis can be seen as their collective effort to redress the balance of their personal fortunes. It can also be seen as the first attempt at political, social and economic reforms to be undertaken in a Gulf state in an orderly and institutionalized – if only semi-democratic – manner. Or it can be seen as the first formal representative government.

Despite the fact that the Majlis lasted for just under six months, the year 1938 is still referred to in Kuwait as the Year of the Majlis. During its tenure, it embarked on a development programme which included a number of important reforms. The educational system was expanded; corrupt customs officials were expelled; rents in Kuwait town were lowered; the use of free labour (*al sukhra*) by the Al Sabah was abolished; legal reforms were introduced; and a disciplined police force was organized.

But some of the essential weaknesses of the Majlis ultimately brought about its collapse. By confining candidacy and membership to the notables, it naturally incurred the resentment of the rest of the population. The Shia were one group in point: they constituted around a quarter of the population, and were made up of Iranians who had immigrated to Kuwait, Hasawis, Baharinah and Iraqis; they were small shopkeepers and boat-builders. Together with the pearl divers, they regarded the Al Sabah as their protectors. The bedouin also remained loyal to Shaikh Ahmad.

The 1938 Majlis had attempted to introduce participation to the political process (and thus to weaken the central authority of the ruler), and to direct the socio-economic development of the country. But its inability to separate the two objectives of 'participation' and 'development' soon led to its downfall. In mid-December 1938, a minor skirmish in Kuwait town provided the ruler with the opportunity to call on his loyal supporters; he was then able to re-assert his power and dissolve the Majlis. The Year of the Majlis was over.

Shaikh Ahmad, determined not to be accused of tyranny, established another council, this time with advisory powers only. But nothing came of it, especially as he retained veto power in it. In the meantime, three events ocurred that brought major changes:

the 1939 White Paper on Palestine, which brought about a temporary lull in the troubles there; the death of King Ghazi; and the outbreak of World War II.

The welfare state

Although oil was discovered in 1938, it was not to be exploited until World War II was over. The first shipment of oil was exported in 1946. A substantial income from oil revenues began to accrue. In 1946, this was $760,000; it jumped to $2 million the next year; and to $5.95 million in 1948. After the nationalization of the oil industry in Iran in 1951 and the consequent boycott imposed on Iranian oil, Kuwait became increasingly important as a substitute source of petroleum. Pumping, extraction and export of oil took place at a furious pace. By 1952, revenues had jumped dramatically to $57 million, and even more spectacular were the receipts of 1953 which reached $169 million. In seven years, then, income had risen from $0.76 million to $169 million.

The developments accompanying this vast windfall were many. A new ruler, Shaikh Abdallah al-Salim (1950–65) was to steer Kuwait into the modern era. In late January 1950, the 65-year-old Shaikh Ahmad al-Jabir died of heart failure and was succeeded by his cousin who had been President of the 1938 Majlis. The date of his formal accession to power, 25 February, is today celebrated as the National Day, for he is considered the father of modern Kuwait. As Alan Rush has stated:[2]

Despite their varying opinions on most subjects, Kuwaitis are unanimous in ranking Abdallah III [Abdallah al-Salim] the greatest of their modern rulers. Calm amid the panic of the Suez crisis of 1956 and the threatened Iraqi invasion of 1961, frugal amid vast wealth, modest amid ostentation, a peacemaker amidst reckless rivals, he achieved Kuwait's safe transition from an obscure old-world shaikhdom into an internationally known, oil-rich state . . .

The expanding oil industry not only provided the receipts of untold wealth, it also had a dramatic impact on the structure of Kuwaiti society and unwittingly created a new relationship between the ruler and his people. As the direct beneficiary of the new income, his great wealth made him completely independent financially. A process to re-formulate the political structure was thus initiated that resulted in the creation of a welfare state and the establishment of a National Assembly.

The traditional economic activities had all but ceased to exist: boat-building and pearling were replaced by the new operations of the oil company, and by the pressing needs of the development projects which were implemented once the oil money began to pour in.

A number of important changes took place. The first of these was the widespread introduction of educational facilities: primary and secondary schools were established, together with scholarships for advanced study abroad. A university was founded shortly afterwards. The transition from a largely illiterate to a literate society was accomplished within a couple of decades. Literacy was no longer confined to the large merchant families. The members of other groupings – the former boat-builders, pearl divers, small shopkeepers – were now being educated.

The second change was the arrival of a large number of foreign workers who were needed for the major construction and infrastructural development which began in the early 1950s and was to continue for the next thirty years. Between 1946 and 1957, a remarkable figure of 9 per cent annual growth in the population was registered; and this grew to 16 per cent until 1965. In 1946, the total population was estimated at around 90,000; by 1957, it had grown to 206,000. It reached 467,000 in 1965, when the Kuwaitis were outnumbered by the non-Kuwaitis, a condition that persists today.

Formal government machinery did not evolve at the same pace. In 1952, there were only four elected bodies based on the old, traditional lines: one each for municipal, educational, health and religious institutions. The elections were extremely restricted: a committee of twelve persons was chosen by the Chief Magistrate (who was Shaikh Abdallah al-Jabir, cousin of the ruler) and approved by the ruler; the members of the committee then chose 1,000 people who could vote for members of the councils.

These restrictions on membership in the councils inevitably caused resentment. At the time many people called for wider participation in the making of what was to become the modern state of Kuwait. The 1952 Free Officers Revolution in Egypt had captured the imagination of millions of young Arabs. It had overthrown King Farouk and the illustrious dynasty of Muhammad Ali; and it sought to change the old order by terminating the British presence and by introducing social and economic reforms.

The quest for political reform in Kuwait during the 1950s marked a new departure. Its protagonists were no longer restricted to the merchant notables who had been central to the Majlis movements of 1921 and 1938. They now included some of the young educated men who had been abroad and had remained abreast of events in the rest of the Arab world; they were also stimulated by the presence in Kuwait of young, politically sophisticated Egyptians, Lebanese, Palestinians and Iraqis, who were working there. The many clubs established at this time were the principal forums of discussion, like: the Teachers' Club (Nadi al-Mu'allimin), where the Kuwaiti nationalists met, and the National Cultural Club (Nadi al-Thaqafi al-Qawmi), to which the Arab nationalists went. The latter were dominated by the personality of Dr Ahmad Khatib who had qualified as a physician at the American University of Beirut and was to become an outstanding member of the National Assembly after independence.

Political participation also became attractive to the newly formed labour force which included workers in the Kuwait Oil Company as well as those in the construction and development projects. The Kuwaiti workers were joined and stimulated by the many foreigners who had flocked to Kuwait in the early 1950s. They formed the Kuwait Democratic League (al-Usbah al-Dimuqratiyyah al-Kuwaitiyyah), a political group which first became active when many of the oil company workers were made redundant after a major construction programme ended; their resentment at having to return to pearl diving in 1950 was expressed in secretly published and distributed pamphlets.

Three different groups of people were now actively interested in more participation: the merchant notables, with their long experience in making representations to the different rulers; the dedicated and articulate intelligentsia, who included both Kuwaiti and Arab nationalists; and the oil company and construction workers who joined the recently formed labour force.

Shaikh Abdallah al-Salim had himself been a leader of the earlier Majlis movement. He was dedicated to the socio-economic improvement of Kuwait, but he was constrained in two ways. First, he was limited by the conditions of his treaty obligations to Britain. Early in his rule, he had reluctantly promised the Political Resident to accept four British advisers. He therefore appointed one each to the Department of Finance and the airport, and two to the customs administration.

British policy in Kuwait at this time had four main objectives that were spelled out in 1953 for the British Prime Minister in preparation for a meeting in London with Shaikh Abdallah al-Salim. They were (a) to maintain Britain's position and influence, (b) to ensure that Kuwait's investments would take place as much as possible in the sterling area, (c) to ensure that Kuwait's wealth would be used to the profit of all its people and (d) to secure as much of Kuwait's trade as possible for British firms.[3]

Having already accepted the four British advisers, Shaikh Abdallah went on to appoint a retired British Indian officer, General Hasted, to be in charge of development. An Economic Development Plan, which called for an expenditure of $400 million over ten years, was put into operation by the newly created Development Board. By 1954, there were around 700 Britons living and working in Kuwait. They aroused the resentment of the population who regarded their many financial privileges as an abuse of Kuwaiti wealth.

In this context, it is interesting to note the American consul's observations about the presence of the British engineers and other technicians who were part of Hasted's team. He wryly remarked that the Britons responsible for the Development Plan were 'turning Kuwait into an Anglo-Indian rest camp. They are living like spoiled aristocrats in luxurious houses . . . built . . . from State funds while the average Kuwaiti finds it impossible to get a power allocation which would give him a single electric bulb in his house.'[4]

At the same time plans were being inaugurated for vague and irrelevant projects. As part of the plan to feed children at school, a machine was purchased at a very high price 'into one end of which is placed a whole sheep and which delivers at the other end hot mutton sandwiches'. Another project involved the building of a clock tower in the town centre on the Big Ben model. All of this was being planned when only 10 per cent of Kuwaiti homes had electricity. Over and above such projects, the more ordinary ones which were implemented showed technical ineffectiveness and poor workmanship. 'Roads have begun to break up within weeks of being paved, valuable machinery is being destroyed for want of care and skill in handling it, half-completed structures are proving unusable for the purposes for which they were intended.'[5]

The second thing which constrained Shaikh Abdallah was the rivalry within his own family. When this became too much for him, he would withdraw to his favourite retreat at the island of Failaka and threaten to abdicate if the infighting continued. Basically, matters revolved around the question of a successor. There were two main contenders: Shaikh Fahd al-Salim, half-brother of the ruler; and Shaikh Abdallah Mubarak, son of Mubarak the Great.

It has been said that there is a tradition that the rulers of Kuwait in the present century have been chosen alternatively from the descendants of Salim and Jabir, two of the sons of Mubarak the Great who had themselves been rulers. This would explain why Ahmad al-Jabir was succeeded by Abdallah al-Salim. But according to Alan Rush,[6] there is actually no hard and fast rule about the succession in Kuwait. The two or three members of the immediate family with the most noticeable personalities invariably become contenders. This was the case of Fahd al-Salim and Abdallah Mubarak. The latter had actually been a candidate to succeed Ahmad al-Jabir in 1950.

Both men held important positions in Shaikh Abdallah al-Salim's administration. Fahd was in charge of the Public Works Department which oversaw the main infrastructural and construction projects central to the development and modernization of the state, and Abdallah Mubarak was the head of Public Security, also a position of great importance. The two men were constantly competing and their followers did the same.

In 1959, Fahd al-Salim died of a heart attack; two years later, Abdallah Mubarak left Kuwait for good, disappointed at not having been named Heir Apparent. After consultation with his family, Shaikh Abdallah al-Salim anounced in 1962 that his successor would be his brother, Shaikh Sabah al-Salim, and designated him Heir Apparent.

These two major constraints contributed to political unrest in a country undergoing change in every sphere. But the economic situation was the most immediate and important stimulus to requests for political participation.

One of the features of the 1938 Majlis movement had been the straitened circumstances of the merchants. In the early 1950s, however, the political arena was not occupied primarily by the merchant notables. They were joined by the intelligentsia and the workers. Together, the three groups had shared in the wealth bestowed on their country. But in the early 1950s, inflation was high (largely as a result of the development policies of General

Hasted), and so a general dissatisfaction with the direction of national affairs set in.

This was exacerbated when General Hasted resigned in 1954. The Development Plan was in the doldrums and the ruler announced that no new projects were to be undertaken until further notice. This resulted in a minor economic depression. Although small in scale, its impact was nevertheless acute, particularly after the extraordinary expansion of the previous three years.

There were two main reactions, both of which were to be repeated in later years under similar circumstances. The first was a generally widespread feeling that Kuwait belonged to the Kuwaitis first and foremost, particularly when there were cutbacks in expenditure. The ruler had already announced that all foreign firms must have Kuwaiti partners in order to operate in Kuwait; these partners of course came from the established merchant community. But now resentment focused on the foreign labour force. The decrease in demand for labour intensified these feelings. The movement for 'Kuwaitization' continued and was finally embodied in regulations which required the discharge of foreigners before nationals. Kuwaiti labour was thus protected by the state.

The second reaction was the desire for greater political participation. Although Kuwait continued to receive the oil money, much less was filtering through the economy because of the virtual stoppage of development work. The merchants in particular wanted to share in planning the future of the state, and resented the fact that members of the Al Sabah had much more influence than they. They petitioned the ruler to call for new elections in the various councils. The results left the merchants in much the same position as before, so they approached Shaikh Abdallah al-Salim personally and explained their grievances.

Shaikh Abdallah responded by establishing the High Executive Committee made up of six members, three of whom were from the Al Sabah. The Committee was given full authority to carry out the administrative organization of all government departments. However, the Amir retained all his powers; the establishment of the Committee was a purely administrative measure. There was no provision for elections to an advisory council, but the establishment of the Committee created a precedent for representative petitions.

In announcing its formation, Shaikh Abdallah made a strong

reference to 'the welfare of our beloved people'. For this was the focus of his policies, and it is clear that he regarded the many economic and social privileges accorded his people as the basis of their welfare, rather than any formal arrangements for political representation. Although the process of re-formulating the political structure had started, its main concern at this time was these privileges, and it was not until the 1960s that the political equation began to change.

The ruler had provided his people with a welfare state, the extent of which was unknown even in the most advanced European countries. His people enjoyed a wide range of privileges, were provided with a myriad of benefits, and were the recipients of a great many state subsidies. Yet no one paid taxes. This fact is central to the new form of welfare state created in the Gulf. The vast income from oil sales was distributed to the people, who, unlike their European counterparts, had made no financial contributions.

Shaikh Abdallah obviously believed in the principle of 'no representation without taxation', and he continued to apply it until the 1960s. His counterparts in most of the other Gulf states, where formal political participation has lagged far behind social and economic development, still adhere to it today.

The National Assembly

Throughout the 1950s, many of the foundations of the modern and welfare state of Kuwait were laid down. Roads were built which linked many hitherto inaccessible areas with Kuwait town; and a good network was constructed connecting it to Saudi Arabia and Iraq. Ports and harbours were expanded. A distillation plant provided 1 million gallons of drinking water a day; the old laborious method of transporting water from the Shatt al-Arab became a thing of the past. Water, electricity and gasoline were heavily subsidized; so too were telephones and many essential foodstuffs such as rice, sugar and meat.

The citizens of Kuwait continued to enjoy special privileges despite their minority status and the continuing immigration. All industrial firms had to be at least 51 per cent Kuwaiti-owned; the same applied to banks and financial institutions. Thus Kuwaiti rights were protected in the face of a rapidly growing market, a narrow economic base and a small population.

Laws were promulgated which restricted citizenship to those and their descendants in the male line who had lived in Kuwait continuously since 1920; naturalization was available only to a few dozen a year and was possible only after a long period of residence. Moreover, naturalized Kuwaitis did not automatically acquire voting privileges; a long waiting period had to come first. In the civil service, Kuwaitis who were university graduates did not have to sit for the otherwise mandatory entrance examinations. They also had priority in the service over non-Kuwaitis and were entitled to various other privileges.

The Kuwaiti therefore felt secure within his own society. Moreover, the government implemented a land acquisition policy whereby it purchased land for development; roads, public buildings, office blocks, schools and hospitals were all built on land acquired by the government. The prices, however, were highly inflated, and many a private fortune was made through sales of land to the state. During the five-year period between 1957 and 1962, $840 million alone were spent; and between 1951 and 1981, a total of $6 billion went towards such sales. Although the ruling family and the leading merchants reaped the greatest rewards from the land acquisition policy, there can be no doubt that they were not alone.[7] Other gifts from the state included interest-free loans for housing to those Kuwaitis who had a low income; and subsidized housing was also available.

It was during the 1950s that Kuwait first became exposed to events in the rest of the Arab world. Hitherto it had remained outside the mainstream because of British protection, its poverty and tiny population, and because many Arab countries were still in the process of obtaining their own independence. With the loosening of British ties and the growing focus of international attention on what was regarded as a modern Eldorado, and with the major changes taking place in the Arab world, Kuwait suddenly seemed unable to resist the force of these changes.

At this time Egypt had the greatest influence, and Nasser's policies began to reach out to the Arabian peninsula. Many references were made to the anachronistic 'feudal monarchies' there and the fabulous wealth enjoyed by their rulers; and also to their continued domination by Britain. The great wealth of Kuwait was a specific focus of the pan-Arab emotions which Nasser revived: this wealth was regarded as belonging to all Arabs, not to just a handful in the faraway Gulf state.

By contrast, and closer to home, Iraq, in close British alliance, was making moves to counter the growing strength of Egypt. After the Baghdad Pact, which included Iran, Turkey and Pakistan in a defence treaty, plans were under way to establish a confederation with Jordan. But to finance such an entity, Iraq turned to Kuwait, which it wanted to become the third member of the confederation.

Shaikh Abdallah al-Salim reacted slowly and with caution. He tried to accommodate his neighbours in Iraq, without however ever committing himself to very much. Towards Egypt, he showed friendship and generosity: during the Suez war in 1956, he encouraged members of his family to demonstrate publicly their support for Egypt, which was being attacked by the combined Anglo-French and Israeli forces. He also granted permission for new clubs – important meeting places for political discussions – to be established in Kuwait at this time; during the 1950s, their number grew substantially.

But in 1959, an event occurred which demonstrated how vulnerable Kuwait was. A show of support on the anniversary of the union between Syria and Egypt (the United Arab Republic) had been planned by the Arab nationalists in Kuwait. Government forces broke up the meeting, many people were arrested and some were deported. After that, political meetings in Kuwait were banned and an atmosphere of tension prevailed.

But times had changed and the situation was not to last for long, particularly where it involved political expression. The July 1958 revolution in Iraq under the leadership of Abdel Karim Qassem had resulted in the overthrow of the Hashemite dynasty there, the establishment of a republic and the termination of a strong British alliance. Moreover, Britain was on the point of ending the relationship it had had with Kuwait since 1899. Its position in the Arab world had altered substantially since the end of World War II, culminating with the Suez débâcle. The anti-British feelings which that evoked were growing in Kuwait, and plans were under way to transfer the control of foreign relations back to Kuwait.

On 19 June 1961, the Anglo-Kuwaiti treaty of 1899 was terminated. It was replaced by one of friendship between the two countries which acknowledged the full independence and sovereignty of Kuwait. Less than a week later, Abdel Karim Qassem of Iraq officially laid claim to Kuwait on the basis of its former – i.e.

before 1899 – status within the Ottoman *vilayet* (province) of Basra. Rumours of an imminent Iraqi invasion had two immediate effects: British forces – acting under a security clause in the treaty of friendship just signed – were rushed to Kuwait; and the Amir of Kuwait witnessed an impressive outburst of loyalty from his people. As it was, the Iraqi invasion never materialized and British troops left before long.

This marked a turning-point in the constitutional development of Kuwait.The Amir's personal popularity and strength provided a strong indication of the state's internal stability. The very fact that there were loyal demonstrations for Shaikh Abdallah attested to the fears of his people that they might lose their valued freedom and prosperity. However they disapproved of specific government policies, they were far from wishing for a republican revolution. Moreover, Shaikh Abdallah enjoyed a good relationship with two of the most outstanding opposition leaders, the Arab nationalists Ahmad Khatib and Jasim Qatami. Shaikh Abdallah set about establishing a political system which would reflect the independence of his people and at the same time refute the Iraqi denunciations of autocracy in Kuwait.

He called a general election to elect a Constituent Assembly whose mandate would be to discuss the constitution which had been drafted by Uthman Khalil Uthman of Egypt. The franchise was restricted to adult Kuwaiti males who had not been naturalized, i.e. whose families had lived in Kuwait since 1920. The demographic construction of Kuwait – together with that of all Gulf states – is that 50 per cent of the population are aged fifteen or below. This meant that only roughly one-quarter of the national population had the vote, a restriction that continues to the present day. The number of voters is always a tiny fraction of the total population. In 1985, for example, these were only around 57,000 out of a total of 1.8 million inhabitants (including expatriates).

The Constituent Assembly was the forerunner of the National Assembly. Those elected to it were predominantly of the merchant community, who had had a long tradition of political involvement. A sub-committee was formed to discuss specific points about the constitution. One of its members was Shaikh Saad al-Abdallah, son of the Amir; the other members were leading merchants. The deliberations over the number of constituencies for future elections was a major bone of contention: the ruling family wanted many, the merchants wanted only one. A compromise number of ten was finally agreed on.

Within a year, the Constituent Assembly had gone through, analysed and amended the draft constitution. Whenever a deadlock arose on a specific point, the Amir invariably urged compromise and encouraged a rapid solution. The Assembly decided that political parties would not be allowed in Kuwait. Other decisions were that the cabinet would not necessarily consist of members of the National Assembly; that the cabinet could vote in the National Assembly, except on a vote of no confidence; and that the cabinet would resign at the beginning of every legislative session.

Once the Constituent Assembly had approved the constitution, the Amir ratified it and it was promulgated in November 1962. Another general election was held to elect the fifty members of the National Assembly. The returns produced deputies from a much greater cross-section of society than had hitherto been the case. They included not only members of the Al Sabah who were cabinet ministers (and as such were *de jure* members) and the merchant notables, but they now also had representatives of the intelligentsia, of whom Ahmad Khatib was a leading figure, the Shia, who were represented for the first time, and the bedouin. The latter two groups, as in 1938, tended to be supporters of the Al Sabah.

But the first major crisis of the National Assembly was about to begin. This occurred in December 1964 over the interpretation of a clause (No.131) in the constitution which stated that a cabinet minister should not hold any other office, profession or partake in business which would conflict with his role in government. When Shaikh Sabah al-Salim, the Prime Minister and Heir Apparent, formed a new cabinet, some members of the Assembly objected to certain ministers on the grounds that they had contravened Clause 131. The Prime Minister found himself in a quandary as to how to proceed, particularly when twenty-six deputies (i.e. a majority) walked out of the Assembly in protest at the choice of ministers. Moves were afoot to persuade the Amir to dissolve the Assembly for being obdurate, but he came in on the side of the deputies: he requested that the Prime Minister change his cabinet.

Less than a year later, in November 1965, Shaikh Abdallah al-Salim died, much mourned by his people. After the accession of his brother, Shaikh Sabah al-Salim (1965–77), the earlier balance achieved between the Al Sabah and the Assembly was no longer as evident. Once again, events in the Arab world had their impact on the political life in Kuwait. The collapse of the United Arab Republic, the fall of Qassem in Iraq, the war in Yemen, which culminated in fighting between Saudi Arabia and Egypt, all contributed to rising tensions in Kuwait. The government became nervous about its ability to maintain peace and order. The Municipal Council, which had criticized the government for abuses of the land acquistion policy, was dissolved. At the same time, many people were arrested and some deported. Although eight deputies resigned from the Assembly in protest against these measures, little change was registered until the next Assembly (1967–71) was elected in 1967.

The results were completely unexpected, for the opposition lost many seats. Reports of government rigging were widespread, and many elected members made statements to that effect. The opposition in the National Assembly, then as today, referred to those members whose stand was usually critical of the government. Since the constitution specified that there were to be no political parties, loose groupings formed around leading personalities; the role of the individual in politics thus became particularly important. Ahmad Khatib and Jasim Qatami were among these individuals. There were now five different groups in the Assembly: the Shia, the bedouin, the merchants, the independents, and the unofficial opposition. The first two were generally considered to be pro-government; the next two groups hovered between the pro-government group and the opposition, depending on the issue at hand. Ahmad Khatib lost his seat in the 1967 election, together with half those deputies considered to be pro-Nasser.

In the meantime, the outcome of the June 1967 Arab–Israeli war drastically changed the position of Gamal Abdel Nasser in the Arab world. Egypt's devastating defeat shocked and subdued his Arab opponents. Kuwait at this time reacted positively: it sent generous financial donations to Egypt and the other front-line states; and many Palestinians from the recently occupied West Bank arrived to take up posts there. The changing order in the Arab world enabled Kuwait to feel more secure internally. It took a neutral stand in the Cold War and was the first Gulf state to establish diplomatic relations with the USSR.

A rapprochement between the government and the opposition

occurred during the next Assembly (1971–5). A number of public issues were raised during that session; and, largely because of the efforts of the deputies, Kuwait gained full control of the Kuwait Oil Company in December 1975.

But the most important event during that session happened as a result of the 1973 Arab–Israeli war, and the spectacular rise in oil prices which followed the Arab oil embargo. The income of the Kuwait government, already immense, quadrupled almost overnight. A boom reminiscent of the early 1950s was registered. The main difference, of course, was that this time the Kuwaitis were enormously rich to begin with, and only became richer. Many shareholding companies were established, and a large proportion of the population became stock market speculators; they continued to be so until the crash of the unofficial stock market (Suq al-Manakh) in September 1982.

The next general election was held in 1975. Once again, the government was accused of manipulating the results, this time by gerrymandering: it was said to have arranged electoral districts to bring loyal voters to the constituencies traditionally held by the opposition. It is interesting to note here that the opposition was much weakened during the electoral campaign by the fact that the two main groups (Khatib and Qatami) were not united in their stand.

However, in August 1976 the Amir suddenly and unexpectedly dissolved the National Assembly; several articles of the constitution were suspended and newspapers were placed under greater control. An important, although unacknowledged, reason for this was the civil war in Lebanon in which the government had unsuccessfully tried to mediate; the government was worried that the uncontrolled Lebanese situation would spill over into Kuwait.

In late 1977, the Amir died. He was succeeded by Shaikh Jabir al-Ahmad (1977–), the present Amir. The tremendous prosperity of Kuwait continued uninterrupted, but once again events in the region had strong local repercussions. The Islamic revolution of Iran in 1978–9, which overthrew the Pahlavi dynasty, upset the balance of power in the Gulf. Moreover, it inspired a wave of Islamic fundamentalism throughout the Muslim world. When the Iraq–Iran war broke out in 1980, it threatened the security of all Gulf states, Kuwait most especially because of its proximity to the battle zone. In the face of the many upheavals, petitions were made to the new Amir to allow the National Assembly to resume its role.

Shaikh Jabir al-Ahmad agreed and called a general election for February 1981. In the meantime, the cabinet had passed a law during the period of the Assembly's dissolution whereby the number of constituencies was expanded from ten to twenty-five; this expansion, of course, had been resisted by the Constituent Assembly in 1962. The new division of the constituencies was said to have lost the 1981 election for all the major opposition groups, who had by now unified their stand.

But new groups had joined the Assembly: deputies who had run on a sectarian (i.e. religious, Sunni or Shia) basis. The new power of revolutionary Iran was reflected in the religious revival and awareness of some Kuwaiti Shia; they ran for the elections as Shia. Sunni conservatives reacted by running for the Assembly as Sunnis. Sunni–Shia differences were reactivated. In previous Assemblies, the Shia had held more seats, but they were generally all pro-government; in the 1981–5 session, they held fewer seats but most of them were sectarian and could no longer be regarded as pro-government.

The next election took place in February 1985. It was in the larger constituencies that the genuine political contests occurred; for in the smaller ones, which could number only around 1,300 voters, the candidates were elected basically as family representatives. It was to this National Assembly (1985–6) that Ahmad Khatib and Jasim Qatami were returned. In an interview with the *Financial Times* on 11 February 1985, Khatib said that to refer to his group as nationalists was a simplification. 'We are rather more than that,' he said. 'We are constitutionalists, democrats, nationalists, and a little bit leftists with rather more interest in the lower income groups.'

The most pressing item on the agenda of the 1985 Assembly was the collapse of the Suq al-Manakh stock market. Its aftermath was particularly acute because of the economic crisis which Kuwait and the other Gulf states were experiencing as a result of the reduction in oil prices. Although the recession was not in any way comparable, say, to that of the 1930s in real terms, none the less its consequences were fairly dramatic. Banks were in trouble, merchants were having liquidity crises, construction work had slowed down dramatically and many migrant workers were leaving.

Another important item was security. The war between Iraq and Iran had made Kuwait very vulnerable. Over and above its physical proximity to the protagonists, it enjoys a remarkably free press; it is also an open society, and one which prides itself on that fact. As in the past, political movements around Kuwait were reflected internally, but this time, they were dramatic, unexpected and deadly. In December 1983, a series of bomb attacks, primarily on American and French interests, brought home the fragility of Kuwait. This was followed in May 1985 by an unsuccessful attempt on the life of the Amir. Six weeks later, bombs went off in two seaside cafés, claiming many lives. Equally frightening was an attack on oil installations in June 1986 when saboteurs almost closed down all Kuwait's oil industry. Explosives went off simultaneously in different places along the pipelines and at the head of a high-pressure well.

This last attack provoked the anger of the deputies, who considered the government to have been seriously lacking in its essential task of guarding Kuwait's one and only resource. They laid the blame on the Minister of the Interior, Shaikh Nawwaf al-Ahmad, half brother of the Amir, and the Minister for Oil, Shaikh Ali Khalifah, whose resignation they had already asked for. They called on the two men to appear before the Assembly to explain the inadequate level of security; they also called on them to resign, along with the rest of the cabinet.

When the cabinet resigned on 1 July 1986, the Amir reacted swiftly. On 3 July, he dissolved the Assembly indefinitely, suspended constitutional provisions for new elections and imposed censorship on the press. Officially, the incident was over. The national newspapers no longer reported the subject, what the deputies had to say, or the possible outcome. A new cabinet was formed less than ten days later. Its composition was an emphatic reassertion of the Amir's confidence in the government: the Prime Minister and all but one member of the previous cabinet were re-appointed. Shaikh Ali Khalifah and Shaikh Nawwaf al-Ahmad returned as Minister for Oil and Minister of the Interior respectively. But the Amir also made a concession to the opposition: five new portfolios were introduced; and non-political men who were basically technocrats joined the cabinet. Four of them had been deputies.

The Assembly has remained in a state of dissolution. There is little doubt in the minds of many, however, that it will return.

When and in what form is difficult to predict in view of the rapidly changing circumstances in the Gulf, particularly those of the Iran–Iraq war. The dissolution in 1976 of the Assembly lasted almost four years. Kuwait is still in the process of evolving a political structure to reflect its socio-economic transformation. Once started, such a process is difficult to halt for a long time.

A spokesman for the cabinet has repeatedly emphasized that one of its most pressing priorities is the economic situation. The economic factor has always been important in Kuwaiti political life. So too have been external events and their local manifestation, when stimulated by internal factors. The agents of change have differed as the society has evolved over the years. The many attempts at participation during the twentieth century have created a tradition that has made Kuwait unique among all other Gulf states.

Notes

1   (Paris, 1980), p. 181.
2   *Kuwait's Ruling Family: Al Sabah. Genealogy and History of an Arabian Dynasty, 1725–1986* (London, 1987), p. 39.
3   Public Record Office, London. FO371/104264: Treasury Chambers to Political Resident, 14 November 1953.
4   National Archives, Washington, DC. R.G 59, 886d.00/3–2053, American Consul, Kuwait, to Department of State, 20 March 1953.
5   Ibid.
6   Ibid.
7   For an interesting study on the land acquisition policy, see Ghanim Hamad al-Najjar, 'Decision-Making Process in Kuwait: The Land Acquisition Policy as a Case Study', Ph.D. dissertation, University of Exeter, 1984.

4 Political Developments in Bahrain

Bahrain is just a few miles away from Kuwait, and its ruling family, the Al Khalifah, belong to the same tribe as the Al Sabah. Like Kuwait, it used to have a thriving pearling industry; indeed, the pearls of the Gulf have invariably been referred to as the Bahraini pearls. It has also been active for a long time in trade and shipping, and consequently has a sizeable merchant community. And it began to receive an income from oil long before Kuwait. In terms of education and technical skills, the populations of both places are the most advanced in the Gulf. Despite these and other similarities, the political characteristics of both places differ substantially.

The political evolution of Kuwait has been marked by a series of dialogues – albeit of varied duration – between the ruler and his people. The pattern of that of Bahrain has consisted of a series of events – accompanied at times by violence – which focused on social and economic issues. The question of political participation has invariably been viewed as a means to attain specific advantages for the population at large. Although socio-economic conditions have improved greatly, political participation still eludes realization.

Bahraini society is not as homogeneous as that of Kuwait. The fact that Bahrain is an archipelago made up of over thirty islands has enhanced the differences between the population; the various ethnic and cultural groups have lived in their own villages, and traditionally do not intermingle, except in the main towns of Manama and Muharraq: these towns have been connected by a causeway only since 1941. The original people of the islands, the Baharinah, are Shia; those of the Utub and their allies, who went there with the Al Khalifah in the late eighteenth century, are

Sunni. Although the exact proportions of the two are not known, it is generally assumed that the Shia constitute a little more than half the population.

The Sunni community is composed of three main groups: the tribes who accompanied the Al Khalifah to Bahrain in 1783; the Nejdis; and the Hawala. The tribes, which include the Al Rumahi, the Al Musallam, the Sudan and the Al Dowasir, are a closely knit community. They used to form the backbone of Bahrain's defence force, but after Britain became responsible for defence they turned to organizing the pearling fleets, and occasionally worked as divers. They did not as a rule engage in either agriculture or trade, but once the pearling industry collapsed, they rather reluctantly became affiliated with the oil industry and certain forms of trade.

The Nejdis left their homes in Nejd (central Arabia) to settle in Bahrain at the same time as the Al Khalifah; they are, however, non-tribal. Some of the well-known Nejdi families of Bahrain are the Al Qusaibi and the Al Zayyani. They are urban and mostly engaged in trade; a number are senior government officials.

The word Hawala is said to have derived from the Arabic verb *tahawwalah* (to change). In the Gulf, this applies to those Arabs who had emigrated to Persia at various times in the past and who then returned to the Arab coast. The Hawala of Bahrain have traditionally been engaged in commerce and trade. Together with the Nejdis, they constitute a community similar to that of the merchant notables of Kuwait. Their names are well known today: the merchant family of Kanoo (who run the Yusif bin Ahmad Kanoo companies, the largest shipping and airline agents in the Arabian peninsula); the Fakhro family, of which the Minister of Education, Dr Ali Fakhro, is a member; and the Shirawis, foremost amongst whom is Yusif Shirawi, Minister of Industry and Development.

The Baharinah by contrast have traditionally been rural people, primarily engaged in date palm agriculture; a few, however, moved to the towns and became prominent merchants. The Al Urayidh is one such family. Some of its members are prominent in the government today: Jawad Urayidh, for example, is the Minister of Health. When the Bahrain Petroleum Company (BAPCO) started operations in the 1930s, many Baharinah became oilfield workers and migrated to the main towns. The introduction of widespread educational facilities also provided the Baharinah with the means to acquire new skills and move away from their traditional occupations. Despite their rural–urban migration over the years, one of their most important cultural and political activities has remained their congregation in the *ma'tam*, a funeral house where the *Ashura* (the commemoration of the Imam Husain's martyrdom) is observed. 'To the Shi'a, the ta'ziyah, which is part of 'Ashura celebrations, and the ma'tam, in which rituals and missionary works are held, symbolize the rejection of worldly power and the forms of government associated with it.'[1]

The Al Khalifah, a branch of the Utub tribe to which the Al Sabah of Kuwait also belong, had originally settled in Zubarah, on the western coast of Qatar, in the eighteenth century. Bahrain was still under Persian occupation. In 1783, the Al Khalifah mounted an expedition against the Persian garrison, expelling it for ever. That same year, they settled in Bahrain. The Al Khalifah therefore became rulers of Bahrain as a result of conquest. Unlike the ruling families elsewhere in the Gulf states, they did not come to power from within the society, an important political difference that may well provide an explanation of the difference between the government of Bahrain and that of, say, Kuwait, namely the absence of a traditional dialogue between the ruler and his people. This does not imply, however, that the Al Khalifah have been unpopular.

Bahrain has had many foreign residents during the recent past, but, unlike the other Gulf states, they have never outnumbered nationals. The largest foreign community has been the Indian, which grew over the years as a result of the long trading association between India and Bahrain. When the oil company was set up in Bahrain in the 1930s, Indians arrived to fill most of the white-collar positions. The fact that they were British subjects and as such had special privileges created local resentment. Another sizeable group of foreign residents are the Iranians, many of whom are merchants. Some have been there for at least 300 years, others arrived during the 1920s and 1930s to escape taxation at home. Although they are Shia, they are separate from the Baharinah with whom they do not necessarily identify.

Two major external forces have had a powerful impact on the Bahraini political fabric. The first has been the Iranian claim to sovereignty, which has been made at different intervals since the Al Khalifah overran the Persian garrison in 1783. With the establishment of the Pahlavi dynasty in the twentieth century, the claim was revived and made with increasing intensity. The presence of a large Shia population in Bahrain served to strengthen the Iranian position. In 1970, following intensive British diplomatic activity, the Shah finally renounced the claim, but the Islamic Republic of Iran has since revived it.

The other external force has been Britain, which for a long period exercised what can be classified as 'direct colonial influence'. With the exception of Oman, the long British relationship in the other Gulf states was confined largely to the control of foreign affairs and was only manifested in heavy-handedness on very special occasions; moreover, interference in the day-to-day running of a state's affairs was the exception rather than the rule. In Bahrain, by contrast, British officials became directly involved in the minutiae of internal affairs.

Since 1869, when Shaikh Isa bin Ali became the ruler, Bahrain came under increasing British influence. Although the official British policy of non-interference in local affairs was occasionally re-stated in London and Delhi, interference there was. A Political Agent was stationed in Bahrain at the turn of the twentieth century; internal affairs therefore were closely scrutinized. In 1915, Shaikh Isa gave up jurisdiction over foreigners in favour of the Political Agent. This strengthened the powers of the Political Agent considerably, particularly since there was a large foreign population in Bahrain.

British influence had evolved in a haphazard manner during the nineteenth century. It was not planned in a methodical manner, and it is doubtful whether any of the officials concerned could have foreseen that Bahrain would become, to all intents and purposes, a British province by the early twentieth century. British interest had originally grown out of the fear that other powers (the Ottoman Empire, Persia, Germany, Russia) would want to establish a claim there. So Britain always remained one step ahead, and inevitably became more involved. Before long, it regarded Bahrain as the most important place, militarily and politically, on the Arab side of the Gulf; and in 1946, the Political Residency, that bastion of British power, moved to Bahrain from Bushire in Iran.

The Bahrain National Congress, 1923

In 1921, a press campaign in Persia began to focus attention on the British role in Bahrain. In view of the long-standing Persian claims to the islands, the British government was keen to become more active there in order to strengthen its position. It was also concerned about being seen to protect the sizeable Persian community, and wished to institute tax reforms which would place the Shia population on an equal footing with the Sunnis.

In 1923, a minor incident occurred which presented the right opportunity for a forward British policy. An argument over a watch stolen from a Sunni by a Persian resulted in riots and unrest. The Political Resident stepped in with measures to restore order. To begin with, he deposed Shaikh Isa bin Ali and installed his son, Shaikh Hamad bin Isa, in his place as ruler. The Resident then introduced a series of administrative measures under British supervision which were to become the cornerstone of the new state bureaucracy. The Customs Department was re-organized with a British director in charge; a Civil List was drawn up and a British adviser to the ruler, C. Dalrymple Belgrave, was appointed. Belgrave, who was employed by the ruler, took up his position in 1926 and was to remain in office for just over thirty years. His autobiography, *Personal Column* (London, 1962), presents an interesting and highly personal account of his long association with Bahrain.

Bahrain was now under firm British control. The enforced abdication of the ruler, together with many of the new regulations, however, created strong local resentment. This was expressed in an *ad hoc* meeting in 1923 of some of the leading opponents of the new order. This became known as the Bahrain National Congress. Its members advocated specific reforms to solve Bahrain's problems: they wanted Shaikh Isa to remain in power and called for the formation of a consultative council to work alongside him; they also advocated the formation of a committee to act on behalf of the pearl divers in order to reduce the prevailing abuses in the pearling industry. In addition, the Congress called on the Political Agent to refrain from interfering in the internal affairs of Bahrain.

The members of the Congress were all Sunni, although its leaders attempted, albeit unsuccessfully, to enlist the support of Shia notables. The latter, however, still viewed their Sunni compatriots with some suspicion, and preferred to depend on British officials for protection.

With little national support to sustain it, and in the face of British opposition, the National Congress could not survive for long. Its leaders were arrested and deported to India. The first formal attempt to introduce participation to the political process was consequently of short duration.

The reform movement of 1938

Although they had been suppressed officially, the aspirations of the National Congress did not fade away; they survived despite British disapproval. In the meantime, an event occurred which has been referred to as the *deus ex machina* of the Gulf. It temporarily relieved some of the tensions which had been building up in Bahrain, but it eventually led to a restructuring of the *status quo*.

Bahrain's first oil well was sunk at Jabal Dukhan (the mountain of smoke) in October 1931, and in June 1932 over 9,000 barrels of oil a day started to flow. This was the first oil discovery in the Gulf. Although with hindsight this strike was very minor – especially when compared with the far more important discoveries yet to be made in Saudi Arabia, Kuwait, Qatar and Abu Dhabi – it was here in Bahrain that oil revenues first began to accrue.

With the help of Belgrave, the British adviser, the government began to divert a large proportion of the income from oil to creating new departments and to laying foundations for the modern state. Bahrain began to enjoy a period of prosperity unique in the Gulf. While the other Gulf states were experiencing severe economic crises, Bahrain became the first oil-rich state.

The educational system, which had originally started as a grass-roots venture at the turn of the century, began to expand quickly. In 1930, for example, there were 600 pupils enrolled in schools; by 1938, the number had trebled. It was not only in the schools that cultural and intellectual opportunities were becoming available. A printing press was installed in 1937, and in 1939 the first cinema in the Gulf was opened. As in Kuwait, a number of cultural and sporting clubs flourished at this time. Employment opportunities, badly needed since the decline of the pearling industry, also became available when BAPCO started recruiting workers.

The new developments inevitably brought about significant changes. As the former pearl divers became oilfield workers, and the date cultivators left their rural surroundings to join them in the towns, the old barriers compartmentalizing the population began to break down. But the transition to an oil-based economy was accompanied by new problems.

In 1936, for example, there had been a brief economic boom when many American engineers arrived to work on the establishment of an oil refinery. Local employment opportunities had increased, and the shops had enjoyed a brisk trade. Once the refinery was completed in 1937, however, a sudden depression set in. Two groups of people were particularly affected: the young educated men, who were unable to find employment at BAPCO; and the merchants, who were on the verge of bankruptcy after shop sales fell dramatically. The newly acquired wealth of the Al Khalifah from oil revenues was in marked contrast to the fortunes of these people, who did not conceal their resentment.

In addition to these problems, the new complexity of government administration began to contribute to a growing gap between the ruler and his people. Whereas previously most Bahrainis could approach their ruler personally with any outstanding problems, they now had to go through the labyrinth of government bureaucracies.

Other important complaints concerned the inefficiency and injustice of the law courts; the ineffectiveness of the educational system, which was not producing graduates to assume jobs either in government or the oil industry, both of which were heavily dependent on foreign manpower; and unsatisfactory labour relations and employment conditions at BAPCO which discriminated against nationals. The last two of these complaints, in short, focused on the importance of the 'Bahrainization' of the oil industry.

Collective grievances continued to grow. They were finally expressed in a widely supported movement which called for reform in 1938, the year when reform movements in neighbouring Gulf states (Kuwait and Dubai) seem also to have been developing. Although the initial demand was for the establishment of a *majlis* like the one recently set up in Kuwait, this was not pursued for long. More specific problems were the focus of the many meetings which took place at this time. These included indirect attacks on Belgrave's omnipotence: references were made to the chaos and inefficiency of the police, the passport office, the prisons, the municipality and customs administration, most of which he directed.

The movement for reform gathered momentum when the

students and oilfield workers joined forces. In November 1938, there were strong rumours that BAPCO employees were planning a strike in support of the reform movement. In consultation with the Political Agent and Belgrave, the government acted firmly to curb the opposition, aware of the trends in Kuwait and Dubai. Two men were accused of being the instigators of the proposed strike; they were arrested and then deported. This provoked widespread disapproval; agitation grew as both sides assumed entrenched positions. A number of opposition societies were formed at this time: the Representatives of the People; the Society of Free Youth; the Secret Labour Union. But they were unable to hold out for long against the combined forces of Belgrave, the Political Agent and BAPCO which dismissed any worker who went on strike. The movement eventually petered out.

But some of its demands were met. The government sanctioned the formation of a national labour committee, and appointed a labour relations representative to the oil company. The government also sought the advice of an educational expert to improve the system and make it more relevant to the needs of Bahrain. In retrospect, therefore, the 1938 movement marked the first major reaction to the establishment of an oil state in the Gulf.

The concessions made at the time were clearly not sufficient to contain the prevailing tensions. During the years of World War II, however, political activity was subdued. The main arena for its expression was in the *ma'atim* (Shia funeral houses) and the clubs. The latter had been established mostly during the 1920s and 1930s as venues for literary and intellectual discussion. They gathered together students, newly-qualified school leavers, merchants, schoolmasters and oil company employees.

Other sources were the *Bahrain*, the first newspaper to be published in the Gulf (1939); and the Bahrain Broadcasting Station, established by the (British) Ministry of Information in 1940 to counteract Axis propaganda. These had a profound local impact; the radio broadcasts in particular had instant appeal for a population still largely illiterate. British slogans concerning freedom and democracy were readily accepted by the people of Bahrain who sought to apply these principles for themselves.

The Higher Executive Committee, 1953–6

After the end of World War II, the first major event to mobilize political consciousness was the Palestine problem. As Kuwait had been the most active place in the Gulf during the 1936–9 crisis, so Bahrain became, once the UN partition plan for Palestine became known in 1947. Some public meetings were held to support the Palestinians, others were devoted to collecting money. And there were demonstrations – peaceful, mostly, except for one – to protest against the partition plan: Sunni, Shia and Iranian alike joined in these demonstrations. Shaikh Salman bin Hamad, who became ruler in 1942 when his father Shaikh Hamad died, sympathized with the people of Palestine; but he did not consider that Palestine affairs called for any action in Bahrain. As in Kuwait, then, a fusion between the anti-government sentiments and the Palestine problem resulted.

During the next two decades, this fusion was sustained, albeit in a different form. The Palestine question was superseded by the objectives of Arab nationalism. The Free Officers revolution in Egypt had the strongest influence. The charisma of Gamal Abdel Nasser, who expressed pan-Arab aspirations, mobilized public opinion and his call for the loosening of imperial control throughout the Arab world struck a resonant note in Bahrain where thousands listened regularly to *Sawt al Arab*, the Egyptian radio station. Although in later years Nasser was said to have had little to do with the events in Bahrain during this period, his impact was unmistakable.

The Political Residency had moved to Bahrain from Bushire in 1946. Its closer links with the ruler, and the increasing influence of Belgrave, provoked local indignation. Belgrave's position as adviser to the ruler had gained considerably in importance. By this time, he had centralized most of the government machinery in his own hands; moreover, his financial and administrative policies were extremely conservative. Different Political Residents had invariably recognized these shortcomings; but they always acknowledged that he was a very able administrator and had the ruler's support and approval at all times.

Pamphlets demanding reform and greater participation were distributed in the streets of Manama and Muharraq. The arena for political development continued to be the clubs and the press which had flourished after the war. A series of clashes from 1953 on between the government and the opposition came to a head in 1956, the year of the Suez war. General frustration with the existing socio-political status of Bahrain became fused with nationalism and anti-British sentiments; these resulted in open defiance of the government. The latter, bolstered by British forces, suppressed all opposition, imposed a state of emergency and forbade all political activity.

In September 1953, serious riots between Sunnis and Shias broke out during *Ashura* (the Shia commemoration of the martyrdom of the Imam Husain). Fear of further sectarian disputes following the heavy-handedness of the police, who tried to disperse the crowd, brought together a group of liberal Sunnis and Shias. They realized that such conflicts only served to weaken society and sought to secure a *modus vivendi* whereby both sects could peacefully co-exist.

In the meantime, sectarian hostilities continued to simmer beneath the surface. Severe riots erupted again in late June 1954. Many were arrested and put on trial. The Shia, however, were convinced that heavy-handed justice had been done: the Shia prisoners, who outnumbered the Sunni, received much harsher sentences; and the judge was a Sunni. In early July, Shia protesters marched to the place where the prisoners were being held; the police, acting without orders, opened fire and killed four people.

Shocked, members of the Shia community went to the Political Agency and asked for British protection, and they declared a general strike. Matters threatened to get out of hand as Sunni tribesmen, traditional supporters of the ruling family, converged on Manama and Muharraq, prepared to break the strike at any cost.

At this point, a group of four Sunnis and four Shias came together and founded the Higher Executive Committee. Its main line of thought was that the basis for the administration of the country laid down in the 1920s, although adequate at that time, no longer suited present needs. Bahraini society had made great strides forward during the past thirty years, but government machinery had remained static. Consequently, a great gap between government and people had developed, and dissatisfaction prevailed. The only way to bridge the gap and thereby alleviate public discontent was to introduce political participation.

At no time was the power or the authority of the Al Khalifah questioned.

Certain functional forms of representative government already existed. Half the members of the municipal council were elected; the other half were appointed by the government. Since the franchise was restricted to property owners, women with property were entitled to vote. There were also councils to handle the *waqf* (religious trust funds); a water and agricultural committee; a council of merchants; and a council for pearl-diving matters.

But according to Sir Bernard Burrows, who was the Political Resident in 1954, the ruler had his own philosophy of government. 'His view is that all would be well if people stuck to their own concerns; that is to say, it is the function of Government to govern, of the merchants to trade, of the farmers to farm and of the workers to work, and the less any of these groups interfere in the concerns of the other the better.'[2]

Generally speaking, the British officials in Bahrain were in two minds about the situation. On the one hand, they recognized that the aspirations of the people were valid; on the other, they did not want to exert any undue influence on the ruler which might have an adverse effect on the security of his position.

After the strike was called off, and acting on the Political Agent's advice, Shaikh Salman appointed a commission to inquire into the causes of the July violence. Compensation for the families of the victims was also paid. But these measures did not satisfy the members of the Higher Executive Committee. They were convinced that only the establishment of representative government would prevent further violence and bloodshed. They therefore petitioned Shaikh Salman to sanction the election of a legislative assembly; to introduce a codified system of civil and criminal law; to permit the establishment of a trade union; and to establish a court of appeal.

The ruler was firmly opposed to the idea of a legislative assembly, but he was prepared to announce the formation of committees to oversee health, education and police matters. The Higher Executive Committee saw this as inadequate and called a general strike throughout Bahrain. This was extremely effective; all work stopped for a week except for those public services maintained by British staff.

As in 1938, both sides had now assumed entrenched positions; Shaikh Salman refused to recognize the Higher Executive

Committee, and the Committee would not endorse any of the compromise solutions offered by the government. A temporary truce was called during elections for an education council in early 1956. But that only made matters worse: the election of some Committee-sponsored candidates was overruled by the government, which dismissed them. The stage was set for further confrontation.

This began in early 1956, during the visit to Bahrain of Selwyn Lloyd, the British Foreign Secretary. Political consciousness had evolved considerably since 1953–4 when Shia and Sunni had fought each other in the streets. Sectarian riots were never again to be repeated, both groups now being represented on the Higher Executive Committee. Moreover, because many local grievances remained unresolved, the opposition made common cause with political events in the Arab world. Nasser's growing conflict with Britain had local ramifications. Thus when Selwyn Lloyd and his entourage were being driven through the streets, their cars were accosted by angry demonstrators who denounced Britain and Belgrave's role in Bahrain.

Tensions remained high and erupted a few days later during a dispute in the market involving a municipal official. Because he was regarded as a government employee, a crowd turned on the official. The police intervened and fired into the crowd; three people were killed and a number wounded. Strong shock waves swept Bahrain. The Higher Executive Committee called a general strike in protest against the killings, and once again all activity in Bahrain ground to a halt.

The time was right for discussion and compromise. With the encouragement of the Political Agent, both sides held a number of meetings. It was agreed that the Committee would drop its demand for a legislative assembly and that the ruler would recognize the Committee under its new name, the Committee for National Unity. It was also tacitly agreed that Belgrave would not remain in Bahrain much longer; he finally left in 1957. The controversial office of Adviser to the ruler was abolished, and replaced by that of Secretary to the government. In 1969 it was in turn replaced by the State Council which after independence in 1971 became the Council of Ministers.

The following months saw a number of tentative attempts to continue to heal the breach, but an external event, the Suez war, brought these efforts abruptly to an end. After the Anglo-French and Israeli invasion of Egypt started, spontaneous demonstrations of protest took place all over Bahrain in November 1956. They were peaceful at first, but later there was some violence. The government quickly assumed that the Committee for National Unity was responsible. Its leaders were arrested and the organization was disbanded. To avoid any protests, the government then declared a state of emergency. All the advances made by the Committee had come to nothing. Another phase in Bahraini history was over.

The National Assembly, 1973–5

The state of emergency remained in force for the next ten years. The press was placed under strict control, and the police force was greatly strengthened. In March 1965, however, another outbreak of violence occurred after BAPCO had made hundreds of employees redundant. The students first took up their cause by going on strike; they were later joined by all the different political groupings which had gone underground during the past decade. They united to form the National Front for Progressive Force which called for a general strike. Riots and demonstrations took place on a regular basis; an open defiance of the police was shown on many occasions as people expressed their frustration and drew strength from the continuing chaos. The cause of the sacked workers was shared throughout the country. Finally, however, the government re-imposed its authority, and the National Front came to nothing.

But once again external events beyond the control of Bahrain were about to initiate major political change. In January 1968, the British government announced the closure of all its bases east of Suez within three years; this included the withdrawal of its political and military presence in the Gulf. Bahrain suddenly had to face the future without British protection. Great fear was caused at this time by the renewal and intensity of Iranian claims, which assumed crisis proportions after the British announcement of withdrawal.

Bahrain was not the only Gulf state which feared the abrupt termination of its relationship with Britain. After having made a futile attempt to persuade Britain to maintain its presence, the rulers of Abu Dhabi and Dubai announced the forthcoming federation of their two states. They then invited Bahrain, Qatar and the other Trucial states to join the proposed United Arab Emirates. For just under two years – from February 1968 to October 1969 – the possibility existed that a federation of the nine states (the seven Trucial states, Qatar and Bahrain) would indeed be established.

But during the course of the conversations and meetings which took place at this time, two major alliances emerged: that of Bahrain with Abu Dhabi; and of Qatar with Dubai. Qatar, which enjoyed vast wealth from its oil revenues, wanted to play a leading role in the forthcoming federation. This was opposed by Bahrain. The two states had a long-standing territorial dispute over Zubarah and the Hawar islands; moreover, Bahrain still regarded Qatar as having seceded illegally. Although Bahrain realized that it had far less money than the three most influential members of the proposed federation – Abu Dhabi, Dubai and Qatar – its own social structure and system of administration and services were much more advanced than any of its proposed partners, and it also had the largest population. Thus, unless it could play the leading role, it preferred to opt for complete independence.

In the meantime, senior British officials undertook a secret diplomatic initiative with the Shah in an attempt to defuse the impending crisis over Iranian claims to Bahrain. After patient negotiation, a compromise solution was reached. In early 1970, the Shah agreed unilaterally to call for a referendum under UN auspices to determine the wishes of the people of Bahrain regarding their future. The results were overwhelmingly in favour of an independent Bahrain. This face-saving formula, which was kept secret and made known only after the death of the Shah, allowed Iran officially to relinquish its long-standing claim to Bahrain.[3]

Having decided to go its separate way, Bahrain then had to develop the requisite political and social institutions. In this, it followed more or less the same procedures as Kuwait. The first step was to acquire a constitution. In an important speech made shortly after independence, Shaikh Isa bin Salman, who had become ruler after the death of his father in 1961, promised that the people would have the necessary framework to participate in the governing of Bahrain.

Shaikh Isa's perception of the constitutional process throughout this period is what Emile Nakhleh has called 'an expression of royal benevolence' rather than 'an admission that the people had any legitimate right to participate in government'.[4] This attitude was borne out during the events which followed the establishment of the National Assembly.

In June 1972, Shaikh Isa decreed that a Constitutional Assembly would be established in December to discuss and ratify the constitution. Like its counterpart in Kuwait, the Asssembly consisted partly of elected members and partly of members who had been appointed by the government. Its job was to approve the draft constitution submitted by the Council of Ministers. The next step was to elect the National Assembly called for in the constitution. The elections by male suffrage took place in December 1973 in a free atmosphere; 27,000 men voted for the thirty members.

Two main political groupings emerged during the short life of the Assembly: the People's Bloc and the Religious Bloc. The People's Bloc was sometimes referred to as 'leftist' since it encompassed Arab nationalists, socialists and communists. It was the largest single bloc in the Assembly and was strongly in favour of such issues as the rights of labour and pan-Arab policies. It had the support of the workers, students and intellectuals, and included both Sunni and Shia. It was, in effect, the political successor of the Committee of National Unity. The Religious Bloc represented the rural Shia, and as such had a generally religious approach to such matters as co-education, the practice of Islamic ritual and moral conduct.

In all, the Assembly had two sessions: the first lasted from December 1973 to June 1974; and the second started in October 1974 and continued until June 1975. During the second session, irreconcilable differences between the government – which was represented in the Assembly by the members of the cabinet – and the People's Bloc emerged. Heated discussions had revolved around the problems of inflation and housing, but two issues polarized both sides: the proposed security bill and the Jufair agreement.

The security bill was very controversial. Shaikh Isa had issued a law in December 1974 which allowed the government to arrest and imprison any person suspected of being a threat to national security.[5] As the only legislative body, the National Assembly regarded this law as an infringment of its authority. Moreover, it emphatically disapproved of the contents of the law; the memory of the events of 1956 and 1965 was still strong.

Another major source of conflict between the Assembly and

the government was the Jufair agreement of late 1971 whereby the US navy had been granted naval and military facilities in exchange for an annual payment of $4 milion a year. Although the agreement was not secret – it had been deposited with the United Nations – the fact that it had not been publicized locally aroused the suspicions of the deputies. Thus when members of the People's Bloc moved to discuss the agreement, the government requested that the session be held *in camera*. After discussion, the Assembly recommended that the agreement be re-considered since it was not in the national interest; the continued US support for Israel was another reason given against it. No action was taken, however, since there were to be only three more sessions of the Assembly before its dissolution. The agreement was finally cancelled in 1977, although the US navy continues to maintain contacts with Bahrain.[6]

With the hardening of positions, it was not long before Shaikh Isa dissolved the Assembly. The cabinet had boycotted the last session of the Assembly, which had therefore had no quorum. The Prime Minister resigned and proposed to Shaikh Isa that the Assembly be dissolved and a new one elected. Although the resignation was accepted, the Prime Minister was asked to form a new cabinet, and in August 1975 the Assembly was dissolved by the Amir. To date, it has not been re-convened.

Developments since 1975

The dissolution of the National Assembly coincided with the beginning of the oil boom which followed the 1973 Arab–Israeli war. The shock of the suspension of the Assembly was absorbed by the distractions accompanying the new wealth which overtook all the Gulf states.

The outcome of the 1973 war marked the beginning of a new phase in the Gulf. The oil embargo imposed by the Arab oil-producing countries made the Gulf states aware that they were not as vulnerable as they had thought in the wake of Britain's departure. Sudden international recognition of their power gave them a measure of self-confidence which was in marked contrast to the vulnerability they experienced immediately after British withdrawal.

Successful negotiations with the oil companies for higher oil prices resulted in the quadrupling of national incomes almost overnight. With the exception of Bahrain, the Gulf states, which were already very rich, were now awash with money. Gigantic development projects of every kind were initiated. The design and execution of these projects, many of which later turned out to be white elephants, were given to foreign companies; they in turn imported a large labour force which transformed the native populations of most of the states – except Bahrain – into minority groups.

Other social repercussions had even more dangerous overtones. The new easy money created a cluster of men in most states whose main ambition became the high commissions which were often the *raison d'être* of the huge projects. Many leading men were thus corrupted, and the backlash was felt throughout the Gulf states and Saudi Arabia.

The emergence of the Shah as the 'policeman' of the Gulf was an important part of US policy in the region at this time. He maintained a good relationship with the Gulf states, having already recognized Bahrain's independence. In 1975, he forced Iraq into a rapprochement which was expressed in the Algiers accord whereby Iran obtained joint control of the Shatt al-Arab river with Iraq. But Iran was also plagued by the same excesses and corruption as were the Arab oil-producing states. Much of the discontent in this vast country was channelled into the religious institutions which thrived undeterred by the dreaded secret police. When the Shah was finally overthrown in early 1979, the Islamic Republic of Iran was established. And with it the revival of Islamic fundamentalism.

The militant government of Iran now began to focus attention on the Gulf states. Bahrain was particularly important to them, because of the old Iranian claims and its large Shia population. Radio broadcasts from Tehran urged the Shia of Bahrain to over- throw their rulers. During 1979, Ayatollah Rouhani revived Iran's claim to Bahrain and actually mentioned the possibility of annexing it.

To the discontented of Bahrain, Iran now became the new source of inspiration, as Nasser's Egypt had been during the 1950s and 1960s. This was manifested in late 1981 when a plot to over- throw the government and establish a republic was discovered and nipped in the bud. It was stumbled across quite accidentally when an immigration officer in Dubai airport noticed irregularities in the passports of some young men who were waiting for a flight to

Bahrain. They were all Gulf Arabs, some of whom had been supplied with military equipment, undoubtedly by Iran, which denied doing so; others had received military training there.

The abortive coup revealed the existence of the Islamic Front for the Liberation of Bahrain, with headquarters in Tehran. Seventy-three men – including Bahrainis, Kuwaitis, Omanis and Saudis – were arrested, tried *in camera* and imprisoned. The government's immediate reaction was to turn to Saudi Arabia for protection. Within a few days, it signed a bilateral mutual security pact with its powerful neighbour. Almost a decade to the day after Britain's withdrawal, Saudi Arabia was called on to assume its role.

Saudi influence in Bahrain had been strong ever since British withdrawal. Bahrain was vulnerable in view of the renewal of Iran's claim and the fact that it was not buffered by great oil wealth. Moreover, Bahrain's relationship with Saudi Arabia was free of the territorial and boundary problems which had beset the other Gulf states. So it was natural that Saudi Arabia would assume much of Britain's old role.

There have been important benefits to Bahrain. The Saudi connection played an important role in the offshore banking sector established in Bahrain in September 1975, a few months after the dissolution of the Assembly. The idea was to replace the Lebanese banking system, which was in a state of decline as a result of the civil war there; it was also important for Bahrain to acquire an economic alternative to its dwindling oil revenue. The venture has proved successful; in 1985, there were seventy-four offshore banks operating out of Bahrain. An important aspect of this success has been the concessions made by the Saudi Arabian Monetary Agency to allow these banks to operate in Saudi Arabia, which gives them a distinct advantage over other banks.[7] Bahrain is well on the way to becoming a service centre for its large and wealthy neighbour.

Saudi Arabia has helped Bahrain in other ways. The offshore Abu Safa oilfield, which is shared by the two countries, provides a large part of Bahrain's income because Saudi Arabia has ensured the production level of the field. Moreover, Saudi influence has been instrumental in attracting a number of Organization of Arab Exporting Petroleum Countries (OAPEC) and Gulf Cooperation Council (GCC) sponsored projects to Bahrain. Some of these are the OAPEC dry dock project which was built in

Bahrain in 1978 (the Arabian Ship Repair Yard); the headquarters of Gulf Air are in Bahrain; and the Gulf University is being built there as well. And in November 1986, a causeway connecting Bahrain with Saudi Arabia was opened. It was financed by Saudi Arabia, and links the two countries even more. The island status of Bahrain has been brought to an end.

The presence in Bahrain of many commercial and industrial institutions, and the relatively small community of migrant workers, has led to the emergence of the largest blue-collar labour force in the Gulf. Because it is over fifty years old, this labour force has acquired certain mechanisms to express demands and grievances; these, however, fall short of the right to strike and to unionization. Labour problems have been an important component of political life in Bahrain since 1938. An outcome of the strikes and unrest of 1938 was the formation of a labour committee, under the chairmanship of a representative of the ruler, whose role was to meet with the management of BAPCO on behalf of the workers. Other similar measures have been taken since then in response to specific grievances expressed through strikes and violence.

A labour law enacted in 1976 (after a major strike at Aluminium Bahrain (ALBA) in 1973) has gone a long way to placing the welfare of the workers on a reasonable footing to pre-empt unrest. The law allows for mediation by the Ministry of Labour in any dispute and for outstanding matters to go to arbitration in mixed courts. In 1981, the eight major companies of Bahrain (Gulf Air, ALBA, BAPCO, ASRY, Bahrain Telecommunications, Bahrain Airport Services, Bahrain Slipway Company and BP Arabian Agencies) were ordered by the Ministry to have joint management–labour committees, the members of which were to be elected to a General Committee for Bahrain Workers. Strikes are still illegal, however, and there are no unions.

The service companies and financial institutions have also created a growing white-collar work force. During the boom period from 1974 on, many young men from poor – and mostly Shia – families worked hard to attain technical and middle management positions. They have moved to occupy a higher place in what Nakhleh refers to as 'the pyramidal and hierarchical political structure of the country. The apex of the pyramid is the ruling family, immediately below which is the narrow but influential stratum of big merchants, businessmen and senior government officials'.[8]

The expansion and flourishing of the middle class also helped to absorb the shock of the dissolution of the National Assembly. During recent years, however, the recession has become a very important issue, for it has resulted in a reduction in government spending, in the contraction of offshore banking and in generally subdued economic activity. For the first time in a decade, Bahrain has an unemployment problem. This is proving particularly problematic in a society with the closest thing to a working class in the Gulf and a middle class which has expanded rapidly during the past few years.

The present economic malaise has inevitably revived tensions. These tensions have been enhanced by the Iran–Iraq war. As in the past, internal discontent is externalized and the threat is perceived as emanating from abroad rather than from any internal source. The continuing frustrations of young Bahrainis with their isolation from decision-making have been exacerbated by economic conditions and have created pressures on the political fabric of the country.

The Political Resident's astute observation in 1954 regarding the attitude of the ruler still holds: that he considers it to be the function of the government to govern, of the merchants to trade, of the farmers to farm; and that all would be well if these groups stuck to their jobs. The Amir's policies at present reflect the same philosophy of government.

Notes

1 Fuad I. Khuri, *Tribe and State in Bahrain: The Transformation of Social and Political Authority in an Arab State* (Chicago, 1980), p. 156.

2 Public Record Office, London. FO371/109815, Political Resident to Foreign Secretary, 25 October 1954.

3 See David Holden and Richard Johns, *The House of Saud* (London, 1981), pp. 276–7.

4 Emile A. Nakhleh, 'Political participation and the constitutional experiments in the Arab Gulf: Bahrain and Qatar', in Tim Niblock (ed.), *Social and Economic Development in the Arab Gulf* (London, 1980), p. 167.

5 Khuri, p. 231.

6 Anthony H. Cordesman, *The Gulf and the Search for Strategic Security* (London, 1984), pp. 583–4.

7   Cordesman, p. 407.
8   Emile Nakhleh, 'Bahrain and Persian Gulf security', *The Impact of the Iranian Events upon Persian Gulf and United States Security* (American Foreign Policy Institute, Washington, D.C., 1979), p. 115.

5 The Political Order

The legacy of the past

Khalid al-Saddiq, the Kuwaiti producer and director, released his first feature film, *Bass Ya Bahr* (*The Cruel Sea*), in 1971. Set in Kuwait sometime in the 1930s, it is the sad and haunting story of a young man's battle against the sea. Desperate to earn enough money to be able to marry his childhood sweetheart and to pay back the debts his father had accumulated after being paralysed by an accident while diving for pearls, the young man joins the pearling fleet as a diver. He remains aboard a pearling boat throughout the season – which lasts for months – struggling against the heat, the discomfort of the cramped conditions, the sharks and the jellyfish. When at last he finds the pearl which could make him rich, his hand is trapped in the oyster shell and his friends cut it off to release him. His system cannot stand the shock of amputation and he dies. When his grief-stricken mother is given the pearl, she throws it back into the cruel sea which has caused her family so much anguish.

The film underlines the role of the sea as the principal source of livelihood and vividly re-creates the harsh living conditions which prevailed in pre-oil days and have now been swept away in the flood of wealth. *Bass Ya Bahr* re-captures the life of a people who have come to terms with their harsh environment, and who have a strong work ethic and stable social relations.

The gloss of material modernity has hidden the essential characteristics of contemporary Gulf society. Underneath the modern structures, the old political order, which was hastily shrouded once oil wealth became available, has remained largely intact. When the pearling industry dominated the political economies of the different states, most members of society had specific roles. The participants' functions at different levels in the industry were well defined – from the lowliest diver and puller to the wealthiest merchant who provided the capital to fund the diving season. They became stratified with usage, emphasizing the highly organized character of this pivotal economic activity.

In the political sphere, the ruler provided the required security and central authority for his people to go freely about their business; in return, they provided his income, from voluntary contributions, taxes and customs dues. Decision-making was conducted on the established principles of *shura* (consultation), which was reached with the leading men of the shaikhdom, but the ruler always had the final word.

This balanced relationship was disrupted when the oil companies arrived. The regular income the ruler received after he signed the concession made him financially independent, but he continued to behave in the same old way. Some reaction to redress the balance was therefore inevitable, and we have already seen how this was manifested in Kuwait and Bahrain in 1938.

Dubai also had a reform movement in 1938. The ruler, Shaikh Said bin Maktum (father of Shaikh Rashid bin Said, the present Amir) very reluctantly agreed to preside over an executive and legislative *majlis* which was in effect run by his cousin. Like the Kuwaiti *majlis*, it was elected by leading members of society. During its short tenure of power (October 1938 to March 1939), it initiated and implemented development projects; these included the establishment of the first schools in the Trucial states. The ruler's income from a preliminary oil agreement signed in 1937 was utilized to finance these and other public projects. Unlike Kuwait, however, the main protagonists of the reform movement were members of the ruling family who wanted more of a say in the running of the shaikhdom. They ultimately fell into the same trap as did the leaders of the Kuwait *majlis*; for in failing to distinguish the difference between participation and development, they weakened the basis of their movement.[1]

Although movements calling for participation in government have existed in the Gulf states since 1938, they have not succeeded in transforming the essence of the old system of rule. This has remained basically the same, despite outward change. The brief surveys of Kuwait and Bahrain presented in the two preceding chapters have shown that their political systems are still based on the central authority of the Amir, and that the present patterns are in many ways a continuation of the older, pre-oil forms of governing.

Institutions and bureaucracies – including the National Assemblies of Kuwait and Bahrain – have formalized and given a modern form to the old institutions. All Gulf states have ministries, departments and parastatals. Government institutions conform to those of other nation states.

A closer look at these institutions reveals that a surprisingly large fraction of the old system of government has survived the process of modernization. The Councils of Ministers provide an apt example of this (see Appendix). They all have a large ruling family representation, ranging from around one-third in the UAE cabinet (nine out of a total of twenty-five) to around half (nine out of seventeen) in that of Bahrain.

A further examination of the cabinet lists will reveal that all Prime Ministers and most Ministers of important 'key' departments are members of the ruling families. The ministries of foreign affairs, defence and the interior are invariably run by relatives of the rulers. In the case of Qatar, a new Foreign Minister has not been appointed to replace the late brother of the Amir, Shaikh Suhaim bin Hamad, who died in 1985; the Minister of State for Foreign Affairs, however, is a member of the Al Thani. An exception is the UAE which has not had a Minister of Foreign Affairs since the distinguished statesman, Ahmad Khalifah al-Suwaydi, resigned in 1979. He was not related to any ruling family, and neither is the Minister of State for Foreign Affairs, Rashid Abdallah al-Nuaimi.

The Omani cabinet is headed by Thuwaini bin Shihab Al Said, the Personal Representative of the Sultan (who is also his cousin) and contains three Deputy Prime Ministers, two of whom are of the Al bu Said. There is no Minister of Foreign Affairs; the Minister of State for Foreign Affairs, Yousif bin Alawi bin Abdallah, is not related to Sultan Qaboos.

Despite some variation, therefore, major 'political' authority has been retained by the rulers and members of their respective families. In the different cabinets it is shared on the basis of *shura* (consultation) with a growing group of men who have either the technical expertise or the social status – or both – that is commensurate with their jobs. The philosophy of the ruler of Bahrain in 1954 – that the job of the government is to govern, of the merchants to trade, of the farmers to farm – appears therefore to apply to all the rulers of the Gulf states today.

New forms of participation

It is clear, then, that the old political system has survived the many changes brought about by oil wealth. One of the reasons for this survival can be found in the nature of the political economies of the modern Gulf states. Muhammad Rumaihi, the Kuwaiti author and sociologist, has discussed the inherent socio-political contradictions of the modern systems of government.

He pointed out that the infrastructure of the states has dramatically expanded as a result of the oil revenues; and that this expansion in turn has radically altered traditional social structures. Despite such changes, however, ultimate decision-making has been retained by the ruling families. He attributed this contradiction to an important and dominant characteristic of the modern Gulf states: '. . . the motive force of the society is not production but the distribution of revenue by the state; actual production of oil is carried out entirely by foreigners, the local population playing a virtually insignificant role in the productive process.'[2]

The author was referring here to the fact that oil was discovered and produced by foreign companies – British, American, Japanese and others – granted concessions in return for royalties. These concessions were terminated in the late 1970s when national oil companies were established. But the actual technical operations on which the process of production relies are still dependent on foreign expertise and manpower.

The petroleum industry provides the Gulf states with a very large fraction of their GNPs. Yet because the governments are not directly involved in the productive process, they have retained the essential political characteristics of the earlier, pre-oil days when the pearling industry dominated the structure of society.

In those days, the technology of pearling was entirely indigenous; the foreign workers who joined the labour force for the pearling season were merely attached to the nationals. The industry itself was therefore technically autonomous, although it did depend, of course, on the international market for the sale of its product.

Although the oil industry has not been integrated into the political fabric of the modern Gulf states, its revenues have induced significant changes. The most visible, perhaps, is the vast array of engineering, industrial and infrastructural projects which have abounded since oil wealth made them possible. These projects, however, have not been generally undertaken by nationals; the bulk of them were planned, designed and constructed (and later operated and managed) by the huge numbers of expatriate workers recruited for that purpose.

Nationals have not therefore been involved in the creation of an urban working class. Rather they have formed a large 'middle' class. According to Tim Niblock of Exeter University, 'The growth of this [middle] class brings out the paradox of oil economies: the increase in production (of oil) leads not so much to the strengthening of the working class as to an expansion of the middle class.'[3]

This 'paradox' relates to the role of the state in the economy, its principal activity being the allocation of funds rather than the generation of revenue. One important mode of participation in government, albeit in a non-politicized manner, is provided by the state for its nationals in the form of easy and privileged access to positions in the civil service. Niblock analysed employment statistics to show that the state administrative sector employs a much higher proportion of the economically active population than in the non-oil-producing countries of the Arab world: 55.9 per cent of the total labour force of Kuwait; 29.3 per cent of that of the UAE; and 26.1 per cent of that of Saudi Arabia. By contrast, the equivalent figure for Sudan, a non-oil-producing country, was only 11.0 per cent.

Further examination reveals that a large proportion of nationals are employed in this sector. In Kuwait, for example, 45 per cent of all economically active nationals are in government service (1984). This is an astonishingly high figure for a state whose very liberal economic policies and free trade are central to its thriving and vigorous commercial community. Moreover, nationals in the civil service enjoy many privileges – in salaries, qualifications and fringe benefits – which are not necessarily available to non-nationals.

The civil service administers the many operations of the welfare state; this partially accounts for its large size. The benefits and privileges accorded the citizens of Gulf states are proverbial. Education, which in Oman began in 1970, is available everywhere free of charge; this encompasses pre-school to post-graduate levels. Even the remotest village now has a school, and all states have a university. Talented students are sent abroad to complete their education and provided with very generous grants. Likewise, medical treatment at home and abroad is financed by the state. Policies which ensure that every national owns his own home have been implemented over the years; moreover, the governments of the different states have been engaged in a process of buying and selling land as part of a plan to distribute wealth. Utilities are provided to nationals at a mere fraction of their cost: these include gas, electricity, water and telephones.

The Appendix shows, moreover, that those departments responsible for the administration of welfare policies – such as the Ministries of Health, Education, Water and Electricity – are not generally headed by members of the ruling families; nor are the Ministeries of Commerce, which are responsible for the implementation of the commercial laws which protect nationals from expatriate competition. Foreigners can only do business by having a partner who is a national; and no foreigner can own more than 49 per cent of any company. The benefits to nationals are evident: all the major industrial and infrastructural projects, the bulk of which have been undertaken by foreign firms, involve a local representative or partner who reaps part of the profits. Some states have gone even further to promote the interests of their nationals. In the UAE, for example, the Federal Agencies Law (1981) stipulates that an agent or distributor working for a foreign principal must be a UAE national or a company that is wholly owned by nationals. In Kuwait, there are no foreign-owned banks.

Modern institutions

The existence of vast state bureaucracies has unwittingly resulted in a distancing of the rulers. In the old days, anyone could speak with the ruler. All that was necessary was to walk into the ruler's *majlis* – without prior consultation – and confer with him about any problem or complaint, no matter how personal. Such informality is rare today. Although the right to approach the Amir still exists, it is obviously more expedient to address the government department concerned. The Amir has in effect been buffered by these institutions.

With the exception of Oman, all the states have replaced the unwritten code governing the relationship between the ruler and his people, as well as their social, economic and political behaviour, with a written constitution. The constitutions may also have been conceived as instruments of independence, for they all proclaim statehood and sovereignty.

The constitutions, which were drawn up by Egyptian legal experts, enunciate the individual's rights and privileges within the existing system of government. The Kuwaiti constitution states that justice, liberty and equality are the pillars of society (Article 7); that private property is inviolable (Article 18); and that all people are equal in human dignity and public rights irrespective of race, origin, language or religion (Article 29). The constitution of the UAE is similar in that it spells out the foundations of society as being equality, social justice, law, order and security (Article 14); private ownership is protected (Article 21); all citizens are assured health care; and personal freedom is guaranteed for all individuals (Article 26).

The constitutions also underline the strong position of the Amir as head of state. Kuwait is described as a hereditary emirate, succession of which is limited to the descendants of Mubarak the Great (Article 4); and the person of the ruler is immune and inviolable (Article 54). Likewise, the Amended Provisional Constitution of Qatar specifies that the ruler must always be a member of the Al Thani. The extent of his powers is spelled out in Article 23: he represents the state internally and in external relations; he ratifies and promulgates laws and decrees; he presides over the Council of Ministers in his capacity as Prime Minister; he has supreme command of the armed forces; he appoints and dismisses civil and military servants; he accepts the credentials of heads of diplomatic missions; he may waive or reduce any penalty; and he bestows honours and medals.

In the past, the Gulf states had no well-defined position within the British imperial framework. They were not colonies, crown colonies, mandates or protectorates; they were simply states 'in treaty relations' with Britain. Likewise today they cannot be described as absolute monarchies or dictatorships; nor are they constitutional monarchies. They are a group of Arab states with a unique political system.

Executive and legislative power in all the Gulf states is retained by the rulers and the Councils of Ministers which they alone appoint. The rulers do not, however, have dictatorial powers. They are bound by the Shariah (Islamic law), by age-old tribal customs and values, and by the process of *shura* (consultation).

But as heads of state, they can wield a great deal of power. And they can intervene at will. The dissolution of the National Assemblies in Bahrain and Kuwait by their respective rulers is a case in point.

Royal benevolence

The Amir can also intervene through the mechanism of government. Here the events following the collapse of the Suq al-Manakh in Kuwait provide an apt example. This unofficial, unregulated stock market, which operated in parallel with the official Stock Exchange, started trading in 1976. From 1978 on, it was housed in the Manakh building in downtown Kuwait; hence the name 'Suq' or 'Market' of al-Manakh. It traded mainly in the group of public companies known as the Khalijiyat (or Gulf companies) which had been registered in the UAE and Bahrain to avoid stringent Kuwaiti government control; many of these were 'shell' companies whose shares were speculatively traded. The Manakh attracted all manner of investors – from the poor and humble to the rich and powerful – in Kuwait and throughout the Gulf. During its brief but highly dramatic life, countless fortunes were made through it in an exciting and effortless way.

Its rapid growth was fuelled by reckless speculators. Students stopped attending classes and employees gave up their jobs – many mortgaging their homes – in order to play the extraordinary market which was producing unheard-of profits. The fantastic level of trading and profits was based on deferred payment transactions. Deferment periods could extend to years, during which time the investor's post-dated cheques entitled him to continue dealing in other shares. Given these conditions, it is little wonder that all spare liquidity was channelled into the Suq al-Manakh. The bubble finally burst in August 1982 when over 28,000 post-dated cheques with a total value of $92 billion began to be called in.

The financial collapse that followed shook Kuwait profoundly. Because so many people from all walks of life had joined the scramble for quick profits, observers have likened the crisis to the South Sea Bubble and the 1929 Wall Street crash. Others have argued that the economic repercussions were as damaging – if not more – than either the Iraq–Iran war or the fall in international oil prices.

Private and public companies alike were affected. Many businesses collapsed and the high rate of inflation which had accompanied the wild speculation now began to be felt. The level of debts was staggering. One of the most outstanding cases was that of Jasim Mutawwa, whose name sprang to prominence after the fall of the market. Mutawwa, a young clerk who had given up his regular job to partake of the bonanza, had been very actively involved in the Manakh; after the collapse, he was reputed to have accumulated a personal debt of around $95 million.

The government stepped in swiftly. To begin with, it paid off all 'small' investors, i.e. those with debts of up to $7 million. In another move, it called for the reduction of the premiums which had been built into the post-dated cheques. But as the dust began to settle, it became clear that the situation was far more complicated than had originally been thought. For the entire financial and economic system of the country had been badly shaken by the ever-accumulating debts and lack of confidence. The banking sector suffered seriously, and property prices, which had fallen during the speculative boom, did not seem able to recover. The government wanted to introduce more radical measures to bail out defaulters.

Generally speaking, there were two schools of thought on how to handle the crisis. The first was that espoused by the government (with the Amir's backing). This advocated the *deus ex machina* approach: that the only way the morass of bad debts could be settled and the national economy built up again was through the massive use of public funds. The National Assembly and a handful of senior government officials did not approve of this. They wanted the implementation of recognized financial procedures to regulate the repayment of debts; they strongly believed that the *deus ex machina* policy was damaging both to Kuwait's financial reputation and to its economic future.

The first school of thought can be classified as royal benevolence, for the policies implemented by the government were nothing short of that. After the National Assembly was dissolved in July 1986, the cabinet made it clear that one of its most important objectives was to improve the economic situation. A few months later, in October 1986, the government announced an overall solution to the continuing problems which had resulted from the crash. Banks were instructed to arrive at settlements with defaulters in different ways according to individual assets and cash flow: those with no assets were to sign ten-year interest-free promissory notes; and those with assets were to sign fifteen-year interest-bearing promissory notes. In the case of the former, those debts which could not be repaid during the ten-year period would be written off. The government, of course, partially guaranteed the losses incurred by the banks. In the meantime, the government bought shares in the stock market to bring up prices and intervened in the property market in a similar fashion.

Before its dissolution, the National Assembly had opposed such measures. Its thinking, as expressed by various members, was that public funds should not be used to bail out defaulters; fears of corruption and the creation of a precedent were just two of the many objections voiced at the time. It was this attitude which forced the resignation of the Minister of Justice, Shaikh Salman al-Duaij Al Sabah, for having claimed compensation on behalf of his young son, who was classified as a 'small' investor.

Others who disapproved were Abdel Latif Al Hamad, Minister of Finance and Planning; and Abdul Wahhab Tammar, Governor of the Central Bank. They disagreed with government policy: Al Hamad resigned in August 1982 and four years later, in August 1986, Tammar followed suit. Their respective successors were members of the ruling family, a strong indication of the new, 'political' nature of these positions, previously regarded as technical. Shaikh Ali Khalifah Al Sabah replaced Al Hamad as Minister of Finance and the new Governor of the Central Bank is Shaikh Salem al-Abdel Aziz Al Sabah.

It is generally accepted that the *deus ex machina* policies had the full backing of the Amir. Government intervention in this case was also the Amir's intervention. The policies implemented were clearly conceived of as political rather than financial.

The handling of the entire crisis reveals how the old system of government prevailed over the institutions established to manage the affairs of the modern state. This was confirmed by a Kuwaiti businessman in a statement given to *The Financial Times*.[4] Salah Marzook stressed that the special significance of the government's attitude was a recognition of the social ramifications of the collapse of the Manakh. 'This is a family affair. It is not a financial package but a political social package.'

Overview

In retrospect, therefore, the role of central authority has survived almost intact. The balanced relationship between the ruler and his people of the pre-oil days was disrupted when the ruler began to receive an independent income from oil. Various early attempts to redress this balance were made in Kuwait, Bahrain and Dubai in 1938. But they failed to introduce full political participation.

As the oil revenues increased, the welfare state emerged. The rulers obviously regard its administration as the principal mechanism through which participation takes place: in the disbursements of state income; and in the partaking of heavily subsidized services. This attitude is strengthened by the fact that they levy no taxes on personal income.

The transformation of a society heavily involved in the process of pearl production to one that is the recipient of the lavish services of the welfare state has resulted in a tacit acceptance of the political *status quo*. The subdued reaction to the dissolution of the Kuwait National Assembly in 1986 testifies to this conclusion, and the disbursement of compensation for the losses incurred in the Suq al-Manakh fiasco reinforces it.

One of the major weaknesses of the 1938 reform movements in Kuwait and Dubai was that their leaders confused the two objectives of 'participation' and 'development'. A similar situation continues to prevail: the adminstration of the welfare state is confused with direct political participation.

External forces have acted as stimuli for the mobilization and crystallization of local tensions for the past fifty years. In the past, the Palestine problem and Nasser's pan-Arab policies played a significant role in the internal development of Kuwait and Bahrain. The influence of the Islamic Republic of Iran since its establishment has already been manifested. And there are the effects of Western – particularly US – involvement in the Iraq–Iran war.

The disruption of the pre-oil relationship between the ruler and his people has yet to be fully redressed. Until this occurs, external events will continue to pose a challenge to the well-being of the Gulf states.

Notes

1   For a detailed study of the movement, including a transcription of the minutes of the Majlis, see Rosemarie J. Said, 'The 1938 Reform Movement in Dubai', *Al-Abhath*, December 1970, pp. 247–318.

2   Muhammad Rumaihi, *Beyond Oil: Unity and Development in the Gulf* (translated from the Arabic version, *Al Khaleej Laysa Naftan* [Kuwait, 1983], by James Dickins) (London, 1986), p. 138.

3   Tim Niblock, 'Oil, political and social dynamics of the Arab Gulf states', *The Arab Gulf Journal*, vol. 5, no. 1, April 1985, p. 43.

4   'Charity begins at home', 3 October 1986.

6 The Ruling Families of Kuwait, Bahrain and Qatar

Because the rulers command positions of such strength, the following three chapters will dwell on the dynasties from which they have been chosen. The points in history at which the different ruling families became dynasties vary; they are all, however, included in *Burke's Royal Families of the World* (London, 1980). Some of the families are related – the Al Khalifah of Bahrain to the Al Sabah of Kuwait, the Al bu Falasah of Dubai to the Al bu Falah of Abu Dhabi – and intermarriage between dynasties does occur at times. But each ruling family has its own inner logic and characteristics.

The Al Sabah of Kuwait

'Kuwait is the Al Sabah and the Al Sabah is Kuwait.' This is often heard in Kuwaiti circles, for it is generally acknowledged that Sabah leadership is an integral part of the modern state. The family controls and regulates government in Kuwait, and in return receives a salary from the state.

The Al Sabah has been likened to a corporation. It is an organization with policies and plans; and it has the means to implement them. It has evolved its own hierarchy which is generally accepted and respected. A Family Council, which meets on a regular basis, has gone a long way towards institutionalizing the dynasty. It is led by Shaikh Salim Hamoud al-Jabir, first cousin of the Amir and a member of the Jabir line; he is not, however, a contender for the position of Amir and as such can remain neutral.

The founder of the dynasty, who also gave it his name, was Sabah bin Jabir, first ruler of Kuwait (*c.* 1752–56). He was a member of the Utub tribe, a branch of the much larger Anaiza tribal confederation to which the Al Saud of Saudi Arabia belong.

During the latter part of the seventeenth century, the Utub, which also included the Al Khalifah of Bahrain, migrated from central Arabia following a devastating famine. After considerable wandering, they finally settled in Kuwait, which was largely uninhabited, with the agreement of the tribes controlling the area. According to the scant historical data available, Sabah bin Jabir was responsible for the establishment of Kuwait town and for promoting its role as an entrepôt on the trade route from India to the eastern Mediterranean and Europe.

From those early days to the present, the Al Sabah have ruled Kuwait. They have grown into a very large family, and the names of Jabir and Sabah have continued down the line. Unlike some of the other ruling families in the Gulf states, their past is free of violence as a means to power. There is only one exception: the case of Mubarak the Great (1896–1915) who murdered his two brothers, Muhammad and Jarrah bin Sabah, Muhammad having been ruler from 1892 until his assassination in 1896.

The constitution of Kuwait specifies that succession is limited to those members of the Al Sabah who are descendants of Mubarak the Great. Traditionally, however, succession has been restricted to the descendants of Salim and Jabir, the two sons of Mubarak the Great who were rulers themselves. Although tension between the Salim and Jabir branches of the family today is inevitable, an orderly succession is equally inevitable. What can be referred to as the corporate behaviour of the dynasty, which is upheld by the Family Council, ensures the closing of ranks whenever necessary.

The exact number of Al Sabah is difficult to assess, although they are known to be over a thousand. They are to be found in a wide variety of positions and occupations. The recent book on the dynasty by Alan Rush[1] reveals the extraordinary diversity of its members. Because their power is almost synonymous with that of the state, a handful wield the greatest authority.

The Amir, Shaikh Jabir al-Ahmad, was born in 1926, the third son of Shaikh Ahmad al-Jabir (1921–50). His mother, Shaikhah Bibi al-Salim was the sister of Shaikh Abdallah al-Salim (1950–65) who succeeded Shaikh Ahmad al-Jabir as ruler. Shaikh Jabir, a member of the Jabir branch, is therefore also closely related to the Salim side of the family. After an early career in Public Security, he became head of the Department of Finance before independence and then moved on to serve as Minister of Finance and Economy. He was responsible for the establishment of the Kuwait Fund for Arab Economic Development and directed the General Oil Affairs Office. After Shaikh Abdallah al-Salim died in 1965, he moved closer to the seat of power; he was appointed Prime Minister, and in May 1966 was officially recognized as Heir Apparent. He became Amir in December 1977 upon the death of Shaikh Sabah al-Salim.

His Heir Apparent, Shaikh Saad Abdallah al-Salim (son of Abdallah al-Salim), is a member of the Salim branch and the Prime Minister. Shaikh Sabah al-Ahmad, brother of the Amir, has been Foreign Minister since 1963. Both men are relatively young (in their forties or fifties), but one of the most influential men in Kuwait is an octogenarian, Shaikh Abdallah al-Jabir. His long and varied political career has included participating in the battle of Jahra (1920); and presiding over the first municipal council (1930) and the education board (1936). Since independence, he has served as Minister of Education and Minister of Commerce. He is not a descendant of Mubarak the Great and therefore is not eligible to become Amir. As long ago as 1938, the Political Resident described him as the 'kingmaker' of Kuwait. He is at present Special Adviser to the Amir, a position at cabinet level which he has held since 1971.

Not all members of the Al Sabah are closely involved in politics. Many have opted for careers in business, in government administration and in the professions for which they have qualified at such international centres of learning as Harvard, Yale, St Cyr and the Sorbonne. The women of the Al Sabah are especially active professionally. They defy the image sometimes propagated by the Western media of the confinement by purdah of the women of the Gulf states.

Amongst the most outstanding are Shaikhah Hussa, daughter of a former Amir, Shaikh Sabah al-Salim (1965–77). Together with her husband, Shaikh Nasir al-Sabah (son of Shaikh Sabah al-Ahmad, the Foreign Minister), she has built up a major collection of Islamic art which is on loan to the National Museum; she is also the main administrator of this impressive collection which she runs on a day-to-day basis.

Another of the very active women of the Al Sabah is Shaikhah Badriah, widow of Shaikh Fahd al-Salim who was Director of Public Works during the 1950s. She contradicts the belief that business in the Gulf is a man's world; a dynamic and very successful businesswoman, Shaikhah Badriah owns and manages a large money exchange house (the GTC).

Shaikhah Suad Al Sabah, Ph.D., is a poetess. She is also known as the author of scholarly publications on development planning. She has studied at Cairo University, the School of Oriental and African Studies (University of London) and the University of Surrey. A fellow academic is Shaikhah Rasha Hamoud al-Jabir; she studied at Birmingham University and then at Yale University where she obtained her Ph.D. degree. She is at present a professor at Kuwait University.

The Al Khalifah of Bahrain

During the second half of the eighteenth century, the Al Khalifah left Kuwait and settled in Zubarah, on the west coast of what is today Qatar. Zubarah is only a few miles away from Bahrain, whose pearl banks they could reach easily. The Persians, who were then in control of Bahrain, however, were very suspicious of the Al Khalifah settlement close by. They mounted an attack on Zubarah which was a disastrous failure. In retaliation, the Al Khalifah, under the leadership of Ahmad bin Khalifah (known later as Ahmad al-Fatih or Ahmad the Conqueror, founder of the dynasty) invaded Bahrain in 1783 and expelled the Persians for good.

That was the beginning of Al Khalifah rule. In the early days, there was little harmony between the successors of Ahmad the Conqueror: his sons and nephews were invariably at odds with one another over personal and policy issues. No hard and fast rule about the succession existed, the most able man generally being the front contender. As a result, the history of Bahrain and the Al Khalifah during the nineteenth century was punctuated by their different attempts – successful and unsuccessful – to seize power. This strife came to an end when Shaikh Isa bin Ali began his reign in 1869.

Since then, the law of primogeniture has been applied: the oldest son has succeeded his father. This principle has now been institutionalized and was clearly set out in the first article of the constitution of 1971.

Shaikh Isa bin Ali ruled Bahrain for a long period. He had a forceful personality and was able to bring stability and order to his family. He was eventually forced to abdicate in 1923 by the

Political Resident, who, together with other British authorities, addressed his son Shaikh Hamad as ruler from that date on. The enforced abdication was never accepted by the people of Bahrain; Shaikh Hamad was regarded as viceroy until his father's death. Any reference today to Shaikh Isa bin Ali's reign pointedly gives its dates as being from 1869 to 1932, the year of his death.

The Amir of Bahrain since 1961 has been Shaikh Isa bin Salman, the great-grandson of Isa bin Ali. The Heir Apparent is his son, Shaikh Hamad bin Isa, who is the founder and commander of the Bahrain Defence Force. In Kuwait, the Heir Apparent is also the Prime Minister; Bahrain does not appear to have the same tradition. The Prime Minister is Shaikh Khalifah bin Salman, brother of the Amir; he has held the same position since 1973.

Bahrain does not have the great wealth of some of the other Gulf states; its petroleum resources are among the smallest in the region. The Al Khalifah are therefore not as fabulously wealthy as some of their counterparts elsewhere. But, along with the people of Bahrain, they are very conscious that theirs was the first Gulf country to embark on the process of modernization. The first state bureaucracy and the first schools (for girls as well as boys) are just two of the many features to which they point with pride.

As a strong expression of this attitude, Bahrain chose to celebrate the bicentenary of Arab and Al Khalifah rule in a very distinctive manner. Discarding the traditional fanfare of military parades and fireworks, it concentrated instead on the long traditions of which it is so proud. In December 1983, a historical conference, whose theme was Bahrain Through the Ages, was organized in Manama to commemorate the two hundredth anniversary of Al Khalifah rule in the islands.

It brought together over seventy archaeologists and historians (ancient, medieval and modern) from Bahrain and other Gulf states, from the rest of the Arab world, the Indian sub-continent, Europe and the USA. For a whole week, the headquarters of the conference became a veritable hive of activity. Scholarly presentations were followed by lively discussions and heated debates, some of which continued well after hours. The subjects included all aspects of Bahrain's past – from the third millennium to the twentieth century – and many sessions were transmitted live on television. The celebrations were not confined to the scholarly conference alone. A number of cultural and historical exhibitions were planned around the same theme.

Two committees planned and organized the conference: a ministerial committee (four members) and an academic committee (five members); each included a member of the Al Khalifah. Shaikh Abdallah bin Khalid Al Khalifah, the Minister of Justice and Islamic Affairs and a dedicated historian with a number of publications to his credit, was one of the moving spirits behind the conference. Shaikhah Haya Al Khalifah was a member of the academic committee. She is a professional archaeologist and the Director of Antiquities in Bahrain.

The Al Thani of Qatar

The Al Thani are relative newcomers as a ruling family. But then, so too is the establishment of Qatar as an independent state. In fact, the fortunes of both are very closely linked; the rise of one has heralded the independence of the other.

The founder of the dynasty was Muhammad bin Thani (1868–76) who also gave it his name. Until then, Qatar had been a dependency of Bahrain since the eighteenth century when the Al Khalifah had settled in Zubarah. The Al Khalifah continued to regard Zubarah, which lies on the west coast of the Qatar peninsula, as their own, even after they moved to Bahrain, and on the strength of that claim, they appointed a governor in Qatar during the nineteenth century.

It was in the eastern villages of Doha and Wakrah, away from Zubarah, that Bahrain faced intermittent opposition from the people of Qatar. In 1867, as a result of a number of incidents which had sought to undermine the Al Khalifah, a massive Bahraini naval force attacked Wakrah whose inhabitants fought back bravely but unsuccessfully. The Bahrainis had violated British treaty regulations by embarking on the naval expedition, so the Political Resident became directly involved and imposed a settlement on both sides. He went first to Bahrain and then sailed to Wakrah.

There he asked to meet a representative of the people of Qatar. This was the first time a British official had had any dealings with Qatar. Muhammad bin Thani came forward to act on behalf of his people: he had lived in Doha since around 1850, and had quickly become a notable there.

(Above) 1. In 1937, water was still being brought into Kuwait in dhows from the Shatt al-Arab; it was then delivered to the townspeople.

(Left) 2. These water towers are part of the complex system – including desalination plants – which provides water in abundant supply to modern Kuwait

(Above) 3. Aerial view of Abu Dhabi in 1958, the year oil
was discovered there, with the ruler's fort in the foreground

(Below) 4. Aerial view of Abu Dhabi two decades later

(Above) 5. Sultan Taymur bin Faisal of Oman in 1919 with
some of the leading men of the Sultanate

(Below) 6. Sultan Taymur bin Faisal's grandson, Sultan
Qaboos bin Said, introducing Queen Elizabeth II to some
of the leading men of Oman at his palace in Muscat in 1979

(Above) 7. The luminous pearl which was the major natural resource of the Gulf states before oil

(Above right) 8. Old and new intermingle in Oman: a satellite tracking station seen through the arch of an old fort

(Above) 9. Old and new intermingle in Qatar: a modern hotel in Doha with traditional craft in the foreground

The meeting with the Political Resident represented a milestone in the political evolution of Qatar. It resulted in a written agreement in which Muhammad promised to desist from maritime warfare and to refer to the Political Resident any disputes that might in future arise with Bahrain. It also implicitly recognized Muhammad bin Thani – as well as the people of Qatar – as being independent of Bahrain. Before he left, the Political Resident made public the new status of Muhammad bin Thani by exhorting the people of Qatar not to 'molest him or his tribesmen'.

This was the first step in the establishment of the Al Thani as a ruling family and of Qatar as a state separate from Bahrain. From that date, Muhammad and his descendants forged a place for themselves and their country within the Gulf region. Their political acumen ultimately paved the way for the rich and independent status Qatar enjoys today.

Muhammad's son, Shaikh Qasim bin Muhammad, found new means to distance himself from the Al Khalifah. In 1871, the Ottoman army occupied Hasa (which today constitutes the eastern province of Saudi Arabia), thus extending the Ottoman Empire to the shores of the Gulf. Qasim bin Muhammad, unlike the rulers of the other Gulf states, was not in treaty relations with Britain and had no means of protecting Qatar from its new and powerful neighbour. So he allowed the Ottomans to station a garrison in Doha; in return, he was granted the Ottoman title of *Qa'im Maqam* (governor of the *qada* or district of Qatar). This at one stroke protected Qatar from lingering Bahraini attempts to reassert sovereignty; and it made him unquestionably the most important personage in Qatar.

But Qasim's independent spirit soon began to chafe against Ottoman restraints and he made it clear that he could not accept their many conditions. In order to subdue him and his people, therefore, the Ottomans dispatched a sizeable military force to Doha in 1893. Qasim was an old man by now, but he still commanded the respect and affection of his people, who rallied to his cause. During the fierce fighting which followed, the Qataris, undaunted by Ottoman military superiority, proved to be courageous and determined. Their determination was well rewarded, for after the first day of battle, it was clear that they had emerged victorious. The Ottoman defeat revealed the courage of Qasim and his men, and established Al Thani authority once and for all.

By this time, Qasim had sensed the impending doom of the

Ottoman Empire. He realized the future belonged to the nascent Saudi Arabia and directed his attention there. After the young Abdel Aziz Al Saud (Ibn Saud) in 1902 took back Riyadh for the Wahhabis, Qasim turned to him as a friend and an ally, sending him tribute and friendly assurances. To cement his friendship, he became a Wahhabi himself. His descendants continue as Wahhabis today.

But after 1913, when the Ottomans were expelled from Hasa by the resurgent Wahhabi forces, Qatar once again became vulnerable, this time to the military superiority of its former allies. For the borders between Hasa and Qatar were undefined and could well come to nothing in the face of Saudi expansionism. British officials in the Gulf were aware of this; the Political Resident, for example, estimated that Saudi forces could easily 'eat up Qatar in a week'. The time was right for Qatar to join the British treaty system.

In 1916, Shaikh Abdallah bin Qasim, grandson of Muhammad bin Thani, signed an agreement with the British government of India which placed Qatar on an equal footing with the other Gulf states (except Oman). All previous ties with Bahrain were completely severed. Shaikh Abdallah was recognized as the independent ruler of Qatar. He was granted the title of CIE (Companion of the Most Eminent Order of the British Empire) and a seven-gun salute. The authority of the Al Thani was henceforth upheld by the foremost power in the region.

The law of primogeniture is not applied in the Al Thani. The succession is therefore not predetermined by the simple fact of birth; it depends rather on the most able and forceful member of the ruler's immediate family. The rulers of Qatar have generally enjoyed an exceptionally long lifespan: Qasim bin Muhammad lived and reigned well into his eighties and his son Abdallah bin Qasim followed in his footsteps. There have consequently been only five rulers of Qatar; and because the rulers lived until a ripe old age, they were able to appoint their successors during their own lifetime.

Shaikh Abdallah bin Qasim was the fourth of twelve sons, but he was his father's choice. Qasim had appointed him as governor of Doha in 1905 in order to give him the requisite experience and authority; he gradually abdicated his powers to the young and vigorous Abdallah. But when the old man died in 1913, his successor encountered serious family-inspired problems which were a portent of Al Thani behaviour. He faced strong opposition from some of his brothers and cousins, who, resentful at having been passed over by Qasim, openly defied the new ruler. They also encouraged lawlessness and anarchy, particularly in Doha, which Shaikh Abdallah at times found impossible to contain. He recognized moreover that the Saudis were deliberately courting his disaffected relatives; he suspected that they wanted to undermine his influence at home in order to place Qatar under Saudi protection.

The opportunity to fight back presented itself in 1935. He struck a bargain with the Political Resident: he signed a preliminary oil concession with the oil company of Britain's choice in return for British protection and official recognition that his son Hamad bin Abdallah was Heir Apparent. This had the required effect, and the ruler was thereby able to restore order to Qatar.

But Hamad was destined not to become ruler: he died in 1948, while his father, then in his eighties, was still alive. By this time, Qatar had started to receive an income from the sale of oil. It was still at a very low level – the price of oil was then fixed at the ridiculously low figure of 4 rupees a tonne – but it was enough to be the source of renewed friction between the ruler and the members of his large family, who wanted a larger share. A period of lawlessness returned, similar to that of the 1920s and 1930s.

Rather than face it all over again, the old and weary Abdallah decided to abdicate in favour of another of his sons, Shaikh Ali bin Abdallah (1949–60). The abdication, which was witnessed by the Political Agent and a large assembly of the Al Thani, was the first public ceremony to take place in Qatar. The proceedings were conducted in the ruler's palace in Doha; a British guard of honour presented arms, provided the bugle call and finally fired the salute.

Before assuming power, and at Al Thani insistence, Shaikh Ali had signed a letter in which he promised that Hamad's son Khalifah, who was still very young, would succeed him. He did not, however, honour that undertaking. In 1960, following a pattern by now well established in the Al Thani, Shaikh Ali abdicated in favour of his own son Ahmad. Once again, the Al Thani gathered together to witness the abdication. At the same time, Khalifah bin Hamad was officially recognized as Heir Apparent and Deputy Ruler.

Qatar had by then become a very rich state. Its oil income was already fabulous, particularly in view of the tiny population – there were at most 30,000 Qataris at this time. The abrupt transition from poverty to extreme wealth took the Qataris by surprise. Unaccustomed to urban ways – Doha, after all, was little more than a fishing village – they were not well equipped to deal with their new-found wealth. This was the era when gold-plated cars were sold to them by unscrupulous dealers who had suddenly descended on Qatar, motivated by the desire to become rich as quickly as possible.

Shaikh Ahmad bin Ali (1961–72) proved to be incapable of steering Qatar through this period. He seemed to have little interest in laying the foundations of a modern state. Moreover, the fact that he was allocated one-quarter of Qatar's oil revenues for his personal use encouraged the extravagance of his life-style. His Heir Apparent was better suited to the role of shaping a suitable administrative system for the development of the young state: he had assumed charge of all financial and petroleum matters, he became the final arbiter in all legal cases, and was instrumental in the formulation and promulgation of laws and decrees issued in the name of the ruler.

The turning-point came after independence in 1971 when Qatar became a full member of the United Nations. It had by then become clear that Shaikh Ahmad was not equipped for the rigours of his position. In February 1972, taking advantage of his absence abroad, the Al Thani unanimously voted to replace him. Shaikh Khalifah bin Hamad (1972–) became the Amir. His Heir Apparent is his son Shaikh Hamad bin Khalifah who is also the Minister of Defence and Commander in Chief of the Armed Forces.

The Al Thani, unlike the Al Sabah, do not appear to have a corporate identity. This could be partly because they are not urban-based; the population of Doha, the largest town in Qatar, was never more than 12,000 before the period of oil production began. It could also be partly because the family is very numerous. Factionalism inevitably occurs, particularly when the different rulers – with the exception of the last two – enjoyed such unusually long reigns.

Rather than close ranks, as would, say, the Al Sabah, the Qatari ruling family have displayed open disregard for the ruler's authority in the past. This resulted in intermittent periods of lawlessness. Shaikh Khalifah bin Hamad, who is in his fifties, is widely considered to be a wise and just man, and deeply involved in the socio-economic and political development of the state.

Note

1 *Al Sabah: History and Genealogy of Kuwait's Ruling Family, 1752–1987* (London, 1987).

7 The Ruling Families of the United Arab Emirates

The United Arab Emirates (UAE) is a federation of the seven former Trucial states: Abu Dhabi, Dubai, Sharjah, Ras al-Khaimah, Ajman, Umm al-Qaiwain and Fujairah. It was formed in December 1971, on the day before Britain terminated all its treaty relations in the Gulf. The federation has a President and a Prime Minister; it also has a Supreme Council made up of the Amirs of the seven states. Their respective positions in the past were subject to considerable insecurity because of the absence of the law of primogeniture. But during the past two decades, succession has been fixed and Heirs Apparent in some cases have been named. Generally speaking, the eldest son of the Amir is now accepted as the successor.

The Al Nahyan (Al bu Falah) of Abu Dhabi

Shaikh Zayid bin Sultan Al Nahyan (1966–) is the Amir of Abu Dhabi and the President of the UAE. As such, he is probably the single most important man in the federation. Moreover, Abu Dhabi is undoubtedly the leading power within the UAE; this is due both to its great wealth and to Shaikh Zayid's energetic role in cementing the relationships between the different rulers.

His family belong to the Al bu Falah (or Nahyan, after the founder of the dynasty) section of the Bani Yas. The latter are a loose tribal grouping – made up largely of *hadar* or settled people, but also including a small bedouin population – that is widely distributed throughout coastal and inland areas and makes up about half the population of Abu Dhabi. Although the Al bu Falah is one of its smallest sections, the leading role it has played within the Bani Yas has been out of all proportion to its size. The various sections of the Bani Yas have always looked to the ruler of Abu Dhabi as paramount shaikh; likewise, until the income from oil began, the Bani Yas have formed the basis of the power of the ruler of Abu Dhabi.

The Bani Yas have traditionally been the main rivals of the Qawasim, the other important tribal grouping in the Trucial states who had opposed the British fleet in the nineteenth century. As the potency of the Qawasim was curtailed by the successive treaties with Britain after 1820, that of the Bani Yas, a land power, began to grow correspondingly. It reached its peak during the rule of Shaikh Zayid bin Khalifah (1855–1909) of Abu Dhabi. He consolidated the power of the Bani Yas and extended his influence and authority over many of the neighbouring tribes.

By the end of the century, Zayid (known as the Great) had achieved for Abu Dhabi a position of unquestioned importance in the Trucial states; it could command respect not only in the coastal regions but in the hinterland as well. In 1905, a significant event occurred under the aegis of Zayid the Great: he called a meeting of all the rulers of the Trucial states in order to solve outstanding disputes. The meeting was generally successful, and although it was not to be repeated for another fifty years, it is today regarded as the forerunner of the federation which Zayid the Great's grandson and namesake has so actively promoted.

Because there was no fixed order for the succession, however, Abu Dhabi went through a long period of instability after Zayid's death in 1909. He had seven sons, the eldest of whom, Khalifah, did not wish to succeed, being content with the role of kingmaker. So the second son ruled for three years until he died peacefully. The next ruler, Shaikh Hamdan bin Zayid (1912–22), the fifth son, was the first in a number whose tenure of power was violently put to an end by a rival member of the family.

His brother, Sultan bin Zayid (1922–6) murdered him and then seized the throne for himself. The apparent reason for the murder was that Hamdan had become oppressive; he had obstructed trade and discontinued the subsidies usually paid to the members of the ruling family. But the same grievances which Sultan had brought against his predecessor were soon to be levelled against him. His brothers were left in straitened circumstances by the meagre allowances he paid them. In their anger, they decided to depose him. On a summer evening in 1926, when he had invited his brother Saqr for dinner, the latter fired on the ruler, killing him instantly.

During his short reign of just over a year, Shaikh Saqr bin Zayid (1926–8) was haunted by the possibility of vengeance by his nephews, Shakhbut and Hazza bin Sultan, who had escaped their father's fate but were unwilling to concede defeat. In the meantime, and according to a pattern which by now had become well established, Saqr began to incur the enmity of his remaining brothers. Of the latter, Shaikh Khalifah was the strongest opponent. Since he continued to have no intention of gaining the throne for himself, he skilfully manoeuvred the demise of Saqr and handed power over to his nephew Shakhbut.

The violence within the ruling family was at an end. Shaikh Shakhbut bin Sultan (1928–66) remained in charge for nearly four decades. Almost immediately after he became ruler, his mother, Shaikhah Salamah bint Butti, gathered all her sons together and made them swear never to resort to fratricide.

Shaikh Shakhbut attained a degree of internal security in Abu Dhabi his father and uncles had never known. In this, he was helped at the beginning by his uncle Khalifah, whose sons and grandsons today enjoy much prestige and power in the UAE. Moreover, the new ruler extended his authority to the tribes whose loyalty to Zayid the Great had been unquestioned, and before long Abu Dhabi had achieved the position of prominence it enjoys today. Much of this was due to Shakhbut's firm rule. He also proved to be determined to extend his influence to the Buraimi oasis (known as al-Ain today) despite Saudi attempts to curb it.

Shaikh Shakhbut also strengthened his power in the coastal towns and villages. But his task there was not so simple, for he had to contend with the forces of British policy against which he was all but defenceless. Unlike some of his fellow rulers in the Trucial states, who were intimidated by threats, he did not bow easily to British power; instead, he steadfastly defied British representatives whenever he was convinced of his own rights.

In 1937, for example, the Political Resident issued a warning to the rulers regarding the awarding of oil concessions: the only company with which Britain would allow them to sign a concession was Petroleum Concessions Ltd (a subsidiary of the Iraq Petroleum Company). Although the US company, the Standard Oil Company of California, which had obtained the Saudi concession, was known to be far more generous in its terms than Petroleum Concessions, most of Shakhbut's counterparts resigned themselves to British power; soon after, most had signed with the company of Britain's choice, but not Shakhbut. He shrugged off the warning as hot air (*hawa*) and resisted for two years before he was finally obliged to comply.

Oil was discovered off Abu Dhabi in 1958 and two years later a similar discovery was made in the mainland. Before long, vast revenues began to pour in, but Shakhbut was reluctant to allow the sudden prosperity to alter the traditional way of life. What he feared most was the disintegration of the social fabric of Abu Dhabi in the face of such an extraordinary windfall. This fear was enhanced by the experience of some of the neighbouring states which had acquired sudden wealth. He valiantly refused to allow the oil money to be spent, despite a well-orchestrated international press campaign against him which ridiculed his attitude; he honestly believed that maintenance of the *status quo* was the only way to save Abu Dhabi.

But he could not hold back the tide for long. In 1966, after a family council decided that change was vital, and with British encouragement, Shakhbut stepped down. He was replaced by his younger brother Shaikh Zayid, the present Amir. After a brief trip abroad, Shaikh Shakhbut returned to Abu Dhabi where he continues to be regarded as an honoured personage.

Before he assumed power, Shaikh Zayid had been the governor of the Buraimi oasis. He therefore brought with him considerable experience in administration. He has a great knowledge of and love for all aspects of desert life; indeed, the success of his early career in Buraimi was based on the affinity he had established with the tribes of that area. Almost immediately after becoming Amir, he initiated development projects for Abu Dhabi; and with typical bedouin generosity, he also provided for his less fortunate neighbours in the Trucial states. By 1970, Abu Dhabi's rate of growth was three times faster than that of Kuwait whose rise to affluence had become almost legendary.

Around the same time as the extent of the oil reserves of Abu Dhabi became known, the British government announced that its forces would withdraw from the Gulf by late 1971. Before the shock of the announcement had had time to take effect, Shaikh Zayid sought an arrangement to provide an alternative form of security for the Gulf states. He met the ruler of neighbouring Dubai to settle a long-standing offshore dispute, and shortly afterwards the two rulers announced the formation of a federation between their two states. They invited the other Trucial states to join, as well as Bahrain and Qatar.

The latter two states, although willing at first to consider joining the federation, ultimately opted to go it alone. That left the seven Trucial states. Of these, Abu Dhabi was undoubtedly the leading power, owing to its great wealth and to the leadership qualities of its Amir. Dubai, next in importance, had different views about the nature of the federation; its location and the great aptitude of its people for business had made it into a bustling commercial centre, and it wanted jealously to preserve its own identity. Despite such problems, however, a provisional constitution was drawn up for the UAE; it gave the greatest share of responsibility to Abu Dhabi and Dubai.

When the UAE came into being in 1971, Shaikh Zayid was the President, a position to which he has since been re-elected. His overriding ambition for the success of the federation caused him to dissolve the Abu Dhabi cabinet in 1973 and merge it with that of the UAE. Since then, he has put all his weight behind the UAE, generously donating Abu Dhabi's oil revenues to federation projects, small and large. He has also been an active supporter of the Gulf Cooperation Council which was founded in May 1981. His Heir Apparent (as Amir of Abu Dhabi) is his son, Shaikh Khalifah bin Zayid.

The Al Maktoum (Al bu Falasah) of Dubai

The contrast between the Al Nahyan of Abu Dhabi and the Al Maktoum of Dubai is striking, particularly in view of the fact that they are both members of the Bani Yas tribal grouping. The Al Nahyan reflect their bedouin roots; the latter have a decidedly urban approach which is directly linked to the geographical location and characteristics of Dubai town.

Dubai is essentially a city state which consists of little more than Dubai town. It lies on the coast between Abu Dhabi and Sharjah. Dubai town itself stands astride a creek which provides good anchorage, making it an ideal place for shipping and trade.

Little is known about the early history of Dubai, which at one time belonged to Abu Dhabi. In 1833, two members of the Bani Yas, Udayd bin Said and Maktoum bin Butti, together with around 800 followers, seceded from Abu Dhabi and settled in Dubai town. Before long, Dubai attained an independent status;

much of this was due to the courage and ambition of Maktoum bin Butti who ruled Dubai until 1852.

The changeover from one ruler to another has generally been peaceful, although there have invariably been disagreements about who should succeed. Cousins, nephews and brothers all competed with one another, but during the past thirty years, this trend has halted. The present ruling family have recently started to refer to themselves as the Al Maktoum, the family of Shaikh Maktoum bin Hashar, who ruled from 1894 to 1906. The rulers of Dubai since 1912 have been his son and his grandson; and the Heir Apparent today is his great-grandson. The succession has been confined to a son of the ruler.

Shaikh Maktoum bin Hashar was a liberal and enlightened man. He was quick to seize the opportunity to develop Dubai when the port of Lingah in Persia went into decline. Lingah had been governed by the Qawasim, who administered it as an Arab principality until 1887 when the Persian government replaced them with Persian officials. It then became subject to the reformed customs administration of Persia, which put an end to the port's free trade. Much of the commercial activity carried on there was gradually transferred across the Gulf to Dubai.

With Maktoum bin Hashar's encouragement, the merchants who had previously lived in Lingah began to settle in Dubai, and others arrived in search of prosperity and free trade. Dubai soon became the main port for foreign goods destined for the interior. The foreign population grew as Persians, Indians and others made Dubai their home. Their descendants are still there, contributing to the cosmopolitan nature of the society. The character of Dubai as a bustling and flourishing trading community was thus established well before the oil era began.

Dubai is unique amongst the Trucial states in that no ruler has ever been violently overthrown. Yet until Shaikh Rashid bin Said (1958–), the present Amir, assumed power, the Al Maktoum was characterized by the existence of an opposition group within the family. Shaikh Rashid's father, Said bin Maktoum (1912–58), had more than his fair share of this form of opposition during his reign. In 1929, for example, one of his cousins forced him to abdicate; and it was only with British help that he was reinstated. In 1934, another attempt – again unsuccessful – was made to dislodge him. And the leaders of the 1938 reform movement were his own cousins.

Shaikh Said had a clever and forceful wife, Shaikhah Hussa bint Murr (known as Umm Rashid, or Rashid's mother) whose talents as a businesswoman were formidable. She owned land in Dubai, engaged in trade, and also took an active interest in the affairs of state. Umm Rashid was an outstanding woman who defied convention by entering public affairs, but never acted against her husband's best interests: she tended rather to bolster his financial and political position whenever necessary.

Her son, the present Amir, gradually took over the reins of government from his father who had been physically weakened by the reform movement. In 1958, when his father died, he assumed power. Shaikh Rashid has been instrumental in encouraging the growth of this dynamic city state whose citizens are amongst the most sophisticated and enterprising in the Gulf, and he is himself a leading businessman. Shaikh Rashid administers Dubai much as he would a large corporation. He often acts together with one of his main advisers, the Bahrain-born Mahdi al-Tajir, who was until recently the Ambassador of the UAE to the Court of St James's.

A municipal council was founded in 1957. Town planning was practised, and in 1965, the first Chamber of Commerce in the Trucial states was established. Other achievements of those early days were the building of an international airport, the evolution of a modern banking system and the construction of the largest dry dock in the world.

By the time Britain had announced its imminent departure from the Gulf, Dubai had become the sparkling Venice of the Arab world. It had a flourishing entrepôt trade and what was reputed to be one of the finest gold markets in the world. It is small wonder, then, that Shaikh Rashid was reluctant to lose the hard-earned individuality of Dubai to the projected federation of the UAE.

He realized, of course, that there was no way that Dubai – densely populated, but tiny in area – could survive on its own once British protection was removed. The presidency of Shaikh Zayid of Abu Dhabi did not make matters easier. There has been a long-standing rivalry between the two places. Its roots probably lie in the fact that Dubai was originally part of Abu Dhabi. It has been strengthened in more recent times by territorial disputes between them which culminated in a war during the 1940s; and by the difference in outlook between the essentially tribal citizens of Abu Dhabi and the urban people of Dubai.

Shaikh Rashid was elected Vice-President of the UAE. But soon after the establishment of the federation, it was clear that he and Shaikh Zayid had significantly different opinions of what the extent of its powers should be. While Shaikh Zayid pressed for a centralized and strongly integrated administration, his Vice-President favoured greater local autonomy for each state.

The first major crisis in the young life of the federation occurred in 1976 when the Amir of Dubai refused to ratify the draft of a permanent constitution (a provisional constitution was still in effect, and remains so today) which would have strengthened the federation and thereby increased Dubai's commitments. The crisis was not really resolved, but certain compromises were reached which averted the threatened collapse of the UAE.

By 1979, the many problems facing the UAE had provoked a much more serious crisis. Popular demonstrations took place in various parts of the country urging a stronger union and a more cohesive administration. Because expressions of support were voiced at this time for Shaikh Zayid, it is clear that Shaikh Rashid was regarded as being partially responsible for the crisis. Following the mediation of members of the Kuwait ruling family, the Amir of Dubai agreed to become Prime Minister of the UAE, which meant, of course, that he became much more seriously committed to the cause of federalism. This heralded the effective incorporation of Dubai into the daily administration of the UAE. This does not necessarily imply that Dubai has ceased to function independently: in 1985, for example, it established its own national airline, Emirates Airlines, in defiance of Gulf Air, which is owned and operated jointly by the UAE, Bahrain, Qatar and Oman.

The death of Shaikh Rashid's wife, Shaikah Latifah bint Hamdan, in 1983, closed a chapter in the history of the UAE. She was a cousin of Shaikh Zayid of Abu Dhabi, her own father (Hamdan bin Zayid) having been ruler of Abu Dhabi from 1919 to 1922 when his brother, Shaikh Zayid's father, murdered him and took his place as ruler. Along with her immediate family, Shaikhah Latifah then took refuge in Dubai. In 1939, she married Shaikh Rashid; it was actually during the wedding festivities that her husband and his father were able to overtake the leaders of the 1938 reform movement and re-establish their authority over Dubai.

One of Shaikhah Latifah's sons will be the next Amir of Dubai.

Following a period of uncertainty over the future, which was made more acute by the prolonged illness of Shaikh Rashid, the Heir Apparent was confirmed as the eldest of his sons, Shaikh Maktoum bin Rashid. His brothers are well known in Britain as the Maktoum brothers whose horse-breeding and racing activities have been highly successful.

The Qawasim of Sharjah

After the General Treaty of Peace was signed with Britain in 1820, the prestige of Sharjah went into decline. Whereas its rulers had previously commanded events in the Gulf, they now became insignificant in the power structure of the region.

During the rule of Shaikh Sultan bin Saqr (1803–66), it seemed possible that the Qawasim (singular Qasimi) might be able to regain some of their lost power. With the help of the inland bedouin tribes, he extended his sovereignty to the Gulf of Oman; there he wrested control of Kalba, Fujairah and other places from the Sultan of Oman. Sharjah was then a relatively large state: it included Sharjah town, Ras al-Khaimah, the inland oasis of Dhayd, and the islands of Abu Musa and the two Tunbs. His people were engaged in pearl diving and fishing in the coastal areas; and elsewhere in the cultivation of dates, oranges, mangoes, and wheat.

But after the death of Sultan, his brothers and sons were involved in endless intrigues to seize control. The result has been that most rulers since then have been either deposed or murdered. This trend has continued: in 1972, Shaikh Khalid bin Muhammad (1965–72) was murdered by his deposed predecessor; and in 1987, there was an unsuccessful attempt by his brother to depose Shaikh Sultan bin Muhammad (1972–).

Throughout this process of internecine coup and counter-coup, Sharjah was reduced to a mere fraction of its former size. It was so weakened by the struggles within the ruling family that it became powerless to resist the secession of two (or even three) of its major areas. Maybe the most significant breakaway territory was Ras al-Khaimah which in 1921 obtained British recognition as an independent state.

The second official secession took place in 1936: this was in Kalba, on the Gulf of Oman. Both Kalba and Fujairah had by then effectively broken loose from Sharjah authority, and both had petitioned British officials for recognition. Although the government of India generally acknowledged that it was the ruler of Fujairah who was better entitled to an independent status, he was not to receive it until 1952.

In the meantime, the Air Ministry and the India Office in London were very anxious to establish an emergency landing ground in Kalba for the route to India of Imperial Airways (later to become BOAC and, still later, BA). The headman of Kalba, himself a Qasimi, refused to guarantee the safety of the landing ground unless granted independence in return. Since the ruler of Sharjah was clearly unable to impose his authority over his distant cousin, and since the safety of the landing ground was essential to the air route, the India Office sanctioned the independence of Kalba. Thus the day he signed an agreement with Imperial Airways in August 1936, Shaikh Said bin Hamad Al Qasimi became the ruler of a new Trucial state.

The ruler of Sharjah, Shaikh Sultan bin Saqr Al Qasimi (1924–51) was deeply embittered by the loss of Kalba to his cousin. He felt betrayed by Britain which had only recently guaranteed his independence and sovereignty, also in return for another air agreement. This agreement was made in 1932 when he had given Imperial Airways permission to construct what was in effect the first airport in the Gulf states. Before signing the agreement, he had encountered much local opposition to the idea of such a foreign intrusion in Sharjah; and since the opposition was led by his brother Muhammad, the ruler of Sharjah became very reluctant to commit himself to such a venture, aware of its incipient danger. In order to persuade the ruler to sign the agreement, the Acting Political Resident promised him in writing that the British government would guarantee Sharjah's complete independence and would do nothing to take away his lands from him.

Sultan's brother Muhammad continued to be a powerful figure in Sharjah. In 1949, when the ruler was taken ill, Muhammad became the Regent and gradually took over the affairs of state. In 1951, Sultan bin Saqr died in London after surgery. His sons were with him at the time, so Muhammad immediately proclaimed himself ruler at home. This was contested by Sultan's son, Saqr bin Sultan, after he returned to Sharjah. A family council decided in favour of Saqr, so Muhammad accepted the decision and stepped down. He never became ruler, but two of his sons did:

Shaikh Khalid bin Muhammad (1965–72) and the present Amir, Shaikh Sultan bin Muhammad (1972–).

In 1965, Shaikh Saqr bin Sultan (1951–65) was deposed by Muhammad's son, Khalid bin Muhammad. The Egyptian historian Salah Accad has claimed that Shaikh Saqr bin Sultan had been overthrown with the help of the British authorities; and that they were motivated by the fact that Shaikh Saqr, an Arab nationalist, had declined British help for the development of Sharjah, preferring to rely instead on the Arab League which was then based in Cairo.[1]

The deposed ruler took refuge in Egypt where he began to plan a counter-coup. In 1972, he murdered the Amir who had deposed him, and obviously hoped to take back his former position. But the UAE had by then been established. It refused to allow Shaikh Saqr to succeed by bloodshed, and banished him once again, at the same time placing Khalid's brother Sultan in the seat of power.

Shaikh Sultan bin Muhammad (1972–) was not the eldest of Khalid's brothers. He was, however, the best educated of them; he is the first Amir of a former Trucial state to have earned a university degree. He is, in fact, a highly educated man. His first degree, earned in Egypt, was in agriculture. Well after he had become Amir, he studied at the University of Exeter in the UK from which he received a Ph.D. degree in 1985. His intellectual inclinations are reflected in his promotion of the cultural and artistic development of Sharjah.

Until very recently, Sharjah was quite poor and depended very much on the aid it received from the federation. During the 1980s, gas and oil reserves were discovered: they are of course only a tiny fraction of those of Abu Dhabi, but they have allowed the state to be more self-reliant. The Amir had earlier promoted the tourist industry; the beaches of Sharjah were converted into holiday resorts for European and other visitors. But his decision in 1985 to ban the sale of alcohol throughout Sharjah had an adverse effect on tourism. Other financial difficulties were caused by the collapse of the Suq al-Manakh in Kuwait; many of the people of Sharjah had invested heavily in the Suq and lost substantial amounts of money after the bubble burst in 1982.

The financial problems of Sharjah were cited as the main reason for the coup mounted against the Amir by his older brother, Shaikh Abdel Aziz bin Muhammad, in June 1987. He claimed that the Amir's preoccupation with his studies and research had caused him to neglect Sharjah's economic welfare. It was reported that Shaikh Zayid, President of the UAE, had supported Abdel Aziz's attempt to seize power in the hope that Sharjah would become more self-reliant and less likely to draw on the federation coffers. But the Maktoum family of Dubai apparently disapproved, and strongly urged the Amir not to abdicate.

The threat of a long drawn-out Qasimi family struggle, compounded by the opposing positions of Dubai and Abu Dhabi, alarmed the neighbouring Gulf states. Their attention was understandably focused on the tense international situation emanating from the Iran–Iraq war, a situation which had been exacerbated by the recent bombing of the USS *Stark*. The problem of Sharjah had to be resolved before it too began to take on other dimensions. Bahrain, Kuwait and Saudi Arabia urged a quick solution. The Supreme Council of the UAE was convened, and a compromise reached. Shaikh Sultan bin Muhammad was formally reinstated, and his brother, who was the Commander of the National Guard, was named Heir Apparent and given a greater hand in the running of Sharjah administration.

The Qawasim of Ras al-Khaimah

When Shaikh Sultan bin Saqr Al Qasimi signed the General Treaty of Peace in 1820, he was alternatively referred to as the Shaikh of Sharjah and the Shaikh of Ras al-Khaimah. During his long reign (1803–66), Sultan appointed his sons and brothers as his representatives in the towns of Sharjah and Ras al-Khaimah. Occasionally, they would try to throw off his authority and declare their independence; but they were invariably unsuccessful, because the ruler was too strong and powerful. However, his successors were not as capable, and in 1869, a forceful governor of Ras al-Khaimah, himself a Qasimi, was able to break loose from Sharjah. He died in 1900 without having appointed a successor, so Ras al-Khaimah was quietly and uneventfully re-incorporated into Sharjah.

The next governor of Ras al-Khaimah, Salim bin Sultan Al Qasimi, was more successful in establishing his own family there permanently. He had previously been ruler of Sharjah and had been deposed. The concurrent weakening of the position of the ruler of Sharjah enabled Salim bin Sultan to increase his own power. In 1907 he suffered a stroke, but continued nominally as governor, with his eldest son Muhammad as the effective leader of Ras al-Khaimah. Muhammad later renounced his position in favour of his brother Sultan bin Salim, who became ruler when his father died in 1919.

Although the British authorities were aware that Ras al-Khaimah was quite independent of Sharjah, they withheld official recognition until 1921. That year, Ras al-Khaimah officially entered into treaty relations with Britain, thus becoming a Trucial state. The new state was northernmost of the Trucial states, extending along the Gulf coast for about 65 kilometres (40 miles) and bordering Oman in the north; Sultan moreover claimed the two Tunb islands (Greater and Lesser). Some agriculture was practised in the hilly and mountainous areas; otherwise, the main occupations in the coastal villages and towns were pearling and fishing.

The long career of Shaikh Sultan bin Salim (1919–48) as ruler of Ras al-Khaimah was stormy and far from peaceful. In 1927, he had a major clash with one of his younger cousins after he discontinued the allowances of his relatives. Sultan was angry when his cousin pressed him for money, so he attempted to have the young man killed. The notables of Ras al-Khaimah managed to save his life, but were unable to prevail on the ruler to give him a regular income. Shaikh Sultan was firm in his refusal, and agreed to spare his cousin on condition he left Ras al-Khaimah for good.

His relationship with the British authorities was an even more turbulent part of his career. British officials regarded him as difficult and mercurial; on occasion they used force to impose their authority and there was little love lost on either side. Sultan was generally aware of his defencelessness in the face of British power, and as a last measure he would flaunt the claim that he owed allegiance to Saudi Arabia, not to Britain.

Having established in 1927 his right to disregard the members of his family, Sultan embarked on a course that was ultimately to bring about his deposition. The fact that his income had never been very great had helped to protect him at first but when he signed a preliminary oil concession in 1945, he no longer had any excuses. In 1948, with the concurrence of his relatives, who had received no share of the concession income, he was overthrown by his nephew, Shaikh Saqr bin Muhammad (1948–).

Shaikh Saqr bin Muhammad Al Qasimi remains the Amir of

Ras al-Khaimah today. His hopes that the discovery of oil would reduce financial dependence on the federation budget have not yet materialized. Ras al-Khaimah's resources do not appear to be large enough, although offshore exploration continues.

His hopes for a discovery similar to that of Abu Dhabi earlier prompted Shaikh Saqr to refuse to join the UAE. He resented the fact that his state would be accorded only a minor role in the forthcoming federation because of its low income and small population, and was convinced that this would change once oil in substantial quantities was discovered.

In the meantime, and on the eve of British withdrawal from the Gulf in 1971, Iran occupied the islands of Abu Musa and the two Tunbs, claimed by Sharjah and Ras al-Khaimah respectively. The Amir of Sharjah at the time, Shaikh Khalid bin Muhammad, had made a last-minute agreement with the Iranian government, which allowed the establishment of an Iranian military post in Abu Musa in exchange for annual payments over a fixed period of time.

Shaikh Saqr of Ras al-Khaimah refused to sign a similar agreement, so the Iranian occupation of the Tunbs which followed was fierce and dramatic. Libya and Iraq reacted strongly to the occupation of Arab islands by Iran: Libya nationalized the Libyan assets of British Petroleum, and Iraq severed diplomatic relations with Britain. But Shaikh Saqr received little help otherwise, and was unable to recover the islands. Because the Iranian occupation had occurred one day before British withdrawal, he fell between two stools.

One of the reasons for the murder of the Amir of Sharjah in 1972 was that he had signed the traitorous agreement with Iran. Shortly afterwards, Shaikh Saqr, by then fully aware of his weakness in isolation, joined the UAE. The backlash of the collapse of the Suq al-Manakh of Kuwait was especially acute in Ras al-Khaimah; since many of the Manakh companies had been registered there, the people of Ras al-Khaimah invested – and then lost – substantially in it.

The Nuayyim (Al bu Khurayban) of Ajman

Ajman forms an enclave within Sharjah and consists basically of the town of Ajman which lies about 8 kilometres (5 miles) north-east of Sharjah town. It is a tiny place of barely 60 square kilo-metres (100 square miles).

The ruling family belong to the Al bu Khurayban branch of the Nuayyim (singular Nuaimi), a large and important tribe which includes settled and nomadic people scattered over a large area. The present Amir, Shaikh Humaid bin Rashid Al Nuaimi (1981–) succeeded his father Shaikh Rashid bin Humaid (1928–81). Although a few rulers of Ajman in the nineteenth century were murdered by their successors, this has not occurred at all during the past seventy-five years.

The Al Mualla (Al Ali) of Umm al-Qaiwain

Like Ajman, Umm al-Qaiwain is a tiny state; its surface area is only around 480 square kilometres (300 square miles). Also like Ajman, it has no oil or gas reserves and tends to rely economically and financially on the federation.

Since 1820, when it entered the British treaty system, Umm al-Qaiwain has been ruled by the Al Mualla (sometimes called the Al Ali). During the nineteenth century, the rulers enjoyed a long and peaceful – if somewhat uneventful – life. This changed when Shaikh Rashid bin Ahmad (1904–22) died of pneumonia: after his death, the state was contested and fought over for seven years, during which time two rulers were killed.

In 1929, Shaikh Ahmad bin Rashid (1929–81) became ruler and remained in power until his death in 1981. During the pearling era, he had distinguished himself as a very successful pearl merchant. He died in his eighties and was succeeded by his son, the present Amir, Shaikh Rashid bin Ahmad Al Mualla (1981–), who is in his fifties.

The Sharqiyyin of Fujairah

Fujairah lies entirely on the Batinah coast of Oman and does not therefore entirely qualify as being a Gulf state. Its distance from the other Trucial states made it somewhat remote in the past, but modern highways link it today with the rest of the UAE. It has a mountainous region as well as a coastal area in which Fujairah town is located. Most of the nationals, estimated to be around 15,000, belong to the Sharqi (plural Sharqiyyin) tribe, as do the ruling family.

Fujairah only became an independent state and joined the

Trucial system in 1952. Until then, it was considered a part of Sharjah, although it first refused to pay tribute as far back as 1866. Its fate has been closely linked with that of neighbouring Kalba, which had also originally been part of Sharjah. Both places were prevented from becoming independent by Britain, which regarded them as part of Sharjah.

Rather than join forces against Sharjah, however, Kalba and Fujairah have always been at odds with one another. An ancient enmity between the Qawasim (headmen of Ḳalba) and the Sharqiyyin was revived during the 1920s, and there was intermittent and sometimes fierce fighting between Kalba and Fujairah. The ruler of Fujairah, Shaikh Hamad bin Abdallah, invariably emerged victorious. He gradually became powerful enough to claim most of the land Kalba once governed, but was not able to obtain British recognition, which was essential to achieving any sort of permanence. In 1936, he bitterly witnessed his old enemy in Kalba become a Trucial ruler in exchange for granting landing rights for the Imperial Airways route.

The ruler of Kalba did not prove to be a strong leader, so during the 1940s, Fujairah reverted once more to being the dominant force. Its ruler since 1938 had been Hamad's son, Shaikh Muhammad bin Hamad, who proved able to win over most of the villages in the area. In 1951, the ruler of Kalba was murdered by the son of the deposed ruler of Ras al-Khaimah. The Imperial Airways landing ground had by then outlived its usefulness for Britain; the state had therefore lost its *raison d'être*. Moreover, the Foreign Office in London, which now administered Gulf affairs, was loath to accept succession based on murder. Kalba was therefore re-incorporated into Sharjah.

The strength of Fujairah, by contrast, had grown to such an extent that in 1952 the British government recognized Shaikh Muhammad bin Hamad as ruler of the Trucial state of Fujairah. He continued to rule until his death in 1975. He was succeeded by the present Amir, his son Shaikh Hamad bin Muhammad (1975–) who was at one time the Minister of Agriculture and Fisheries of the UAE.

Note

1   Salah Accad, *Al-Tayyarat al-Siyassiyah fil Khalij al-Arabi (Political Currents in the Arabian Gulf)* (Cairo, 1974), p. 291.

8　The Ruling Family of Oman

In November 1985, Oman celebrated the fifteenth anniversary of the accession to power of its ruler, Sultan Qaboos bin Said Al bu Said (1970–). It was timed to coincide with his birthday which is also Oman's national day. The preparations for the occasion had been under way for two years.

One of its major landmarks was a hotel complex built especially for the occasion; at a cost of $1 million per room, it has been described as a palace straight out of the *Arabian Nights*. The celebrations included all the usual panoply: military parades, fly-pasts, boat races and fireworks; and 5 million light bulbs in the Omani colours of red, green and white were lit in the streets of Muscat, the capital. Representatives from fifty countries travelled thousands of miles to attend the festivities. The last of the celebrations took place in December 1985 when the London Symphony Orchestra was flown out to Muscat to perform works by Omani composers; this was of great personal importance to the Sultan, who is a keen musician.

These celebrations were viewed with quiet disapproval by many in the rest of the Gulf states; they clearly did not think that the prevailing economic atmosphere warranted such lavishness. In fact, it can be said that until Oman joined the Gulf Cooperation Council, it had little in common with its fellow members.

Its geographical location and characteristics are markedly different. Only its northernmost tip, Ras Musandam, lies on the Gulf from where it commands the Straits of Hormuz, the narrow entrance (40 kilometres, or around 25 miles) to the waters of the Gulf. The rest of the large country (of approximately 300,000 square kilometres, or 187,500 square miles) borders the Gulf of Oman and consists of the inland Hajar mountain range; the coastal areas which stretch over 1,600 kilometres (1,000 miles) from the Gulf to the Gulf of Oman, the Arabian Sea and beyond to the

Indian Ocean; and the sands of the great desert of the Rub al-Khali (the Empty Quarter). Such a vast expanse of desert inevitably acts as a barrier to the rest of the Arabian peninsula, at the same time making the country focus instead on the sea, which has played such an important role in Oman's past. The strongest influence on the social and political development of Oman through the ages may have been the interaction between the inland and coastal areas.

Another important difference is religion. Most Omanis – particularly those in the interior – are Ibadis, which are a branch of the oldest sect in Islam. Because the Ibadis are outside mainstream Islamic society – elsewhere they are only to be found in parts of North and East Africa – this has tended to isolate the country further.

The leadership in Ibadism is vested in an elected Imam (spiritual leader). The traditional headquarters of the Imam in Oman were in the inland oasis of Nizwa, in the Jabal Akhdar (green mountain) plateau, several thousand metres above sea level. The early development of Oman, therefore, centred around the interior of the country. The coastal areas did not come into their own until the establishment of the Al bu Said dynasty.

Ahmad bin Said (c.1744–83), the founder of the dynasty, had been governor of Sohar on the coast from where he mounted a campaign to defeat and expel the occupying Persian forces from Oman for ever. He was subsequently elected Imam, and ruled over Oman until his death in 1783. His son Said bin Ahmad succeeded him, but ruled for only a year; he was deposed by his own son, Hamad bin Said. Hamad moved his headquarters to Muscat town on the northern coast, but his deposed father remained at Nizwa and retained the title of Imam. This split between the interior and the coast became stratified with time. The title of Sayyid (lord) of Oman became that of the ruler of the Al bu Said in Muscat; that of Imam, because he was elected, also remained as a more spiritual title for the interior. During the British period, the title of Sayyid was changed to Sultan, which was more in keeping with the spirit of the Raj, and the name of the country was then officially known as Muscat and Oman. It was not until Sultan Qaboos came to power that the name reverted to Oman.

Hamad's move to Muscat heralded the rise of the coastal areas under the Al bu Said, who proceeded to extend their rule to parts of present-day Pakistan, the UAE, Bahrain, Iran and Tanzania. It also marked the beginning of the schism between the interior and the coast, a major theme in Omani politics until very recently. The separation of the two was symbolized by the existence of two rulers: one was the Sayyid of Oman; and the other was the Imam, the religio-political leader of the interior.

The high point of the Al bu Said (and consequently of Oman) was attained by Said bin Sultan (1806–56), one of the greatest Arab rulers of the nineteenth century. After consolidating his position at home, he began to expand the commercial fortunes of Oman. From 1820 on, he was instrumental in establishing a maritime empire which extended from east Africa in the west to Gwadur (a coastal enclave in present-day Pakistan) in the east. This empire was based on an extensive fleet of commercial sailing vessels, which, at the height of its fortune, reached Marseilles and New York. At this time Omani shipping was dominant in the Indian Ocean and contributed substantially to the role of Oman as an important entrepôt for commercial goods.

Said bin Sultan's most important possession was Zanzibar in east Africa to which eventually he moved his residence. An account of life in Said's court in Zanzibar was provided by his daughter in her autobiography, *Memoirs of an Arabian Princess* (first published in 1888; reprinted London, 1980). The story of Princess Salme bint Said bin Sultan of Oman and Zanzibar is in itself a fascinating one. Born and brought up in Zanzibar, she fell in love with Heinrich Ruete, a young German who worked at the German consulate, married him and moved to Europe. She changed her name to Emily Said-Ruete and wrote an interesting first-hand account of the great Omani empire.

After Said bin Sultan's death in 1856, the fortunes of Oman declined rapidly. One reason was the feuding of his two sons, for each of whom the father had designated a specific role: one as ruler of Oman, the other as ruler of Zanzibar. The British government of India was ultimately brought in as arbiter and made what was known as the Canning Award (1861) which ruled on the separation of the former empire into two different states, Zanzibar and Oman.

Another reason for the decline of the Omani empire was the introduction of the European steamships, all but putting an end to Omani shipping activities. This caused the rapid demise of Muscat as an entrepôt. At around the same time, the opening of the Suez Canal stimulated the growth of European steamship lines with which Omani sailing vessels could not compete. The economic hardship to Oman caused by the truncation of its east African territories and by the decline of its shipping and commercial activities was reflected before long in the weakness of the political leadership of the country, vested in the Sultan.

This brought about an inevitable rise of the hitherto dormant forces of the interior: a rival member of the Al bu Said was elected Imam, and within a short time he descended from the mountains to the coast, capturing Muscat in 1868. But he was unable to hold the entire country together without what became known as the Zanzibar Subsidy: the money which, according to the terms of the Canning Award, Zanzibar had to pay Oman every year to make up for its loss. Zanzibar defaulted on the annual payments, and so the British government of India took it over; it was later to be paid by the Foreign Office in London and was discontinued only in 1970.

So the Sultan in Muscat, reinforced by the funds of the Zanzibar Subsidy and with the blessing of Britain, took back the reins of power from the forces of the Imam. The dichotomy between the interior – personified in the Imam – and the coastal areas – under the Sultan – had by now become a permanent feature of Oman: one was known as the Imamate, the other the Sultanate. This split so weakened the country that the British government of India became increasingly involved in the running of Muscat affairs, i.e. of the Sultanate.

One of the consequences was that in 1891 the Sultan signed a non-alienation bond with Britain whereby he undertook never to sign, lease or lend any part of his territory to any power other than Britain. The once-proud empire of Said bin Sultan had shrivelled to a point which made it equal with the tiny Trucial shaikhdoms of Ajman and Umm al-Qaiwain.

It was Sultan Faisal bin Turki (1888–1913) who signed the bond. He had come to power with the help of the British authorities after the death of his father. He soon became involved with French and Russian attempts to gain a foothold in Oman as a direct challenge to Britain's position in the Gulf region. In order to eliminate any such possibility, British officials took the Sultan aboard a British cruiser off Muscat, where they issued him with an ultimatum: he was told to revoke any promises made to France, otherwise they would bomb Muscat immediately. He capitulated, of course.

His son, Sultan Taymur bin Faisal (1913–32) succeeded him very reluctantly, aware that the position was hardly one of wealth, glamour or power. This was made manifestly clear when he was obliged to sign the non-alienation bond his father had signed before, together with a new document which emphasized the weakness of his position. This took the form of a letter to the British government in which he said that: '. . . it is not hidden from me that I shall endure in my rule by the continuance of their [the British government] help and assistance to me . . . and that I rely on the help of the [British] Government and declare that . . . I will be guided by its views in important matters.'[1]

The declining power of the Sultan was made glaringly obvious in 1920. That year, the (British) Political Agent negotiated a peace agreement with the Imam of the interior on behalf of Sultan Taymur; the encroachment of the forces of the Imam had become so marked that the Sultan and the territory he ruled were reduced to a pathetic vestige of their former glory. The Sultan's economic dependence on Britain in the face of continuing poverty led to the erosion of his authority. The Sultan had played no part in the 1920 peace agreement with the Imam; the fact that it had been negotiated by a British official further diminished his stature. By now, Britain was directly involved in the running of the Sultan's affairs; his country, however, unlike the other Gulf states, remained a sovereign, independent state according to international law, but the only foreign representative stationed there was British.

Britain imposed a series of administrative reforms, much as it had in Bahrain. The main focus of the reforms was to alleviate depressed economic conditions. A (British) Financial Adviser to the Sultan was appointed in 1925; he was Bertram Thomas, the explorer, whose rank was then elevated to that of *wazir* (Minister). The customs department was also re-organized under British auspices, but the fortunes of Oman did not improve; to remain solvent, the country had to depend on the Zanzibar Subsidy.

Sultan Taymur bin Faisal continued reluctantly as ruler until he was able to prevail on the British authorities to allow him to abdicate. He left Oman shortly afterwards and spent the rest of his life as a commoner, living in different parts of the east – Singapore, Japan and India. He died in Bombay in 1965.

His son, Said bin Taymur (1932–70) inherited a poor country, only a small portion of which he controlled. Although a young man when he succeeded his father, he had come to the position with some administrative and executive experience; for his father had delegated most responsibilities to his son during the last three years of his reign. Like his father before him, Sultan Said bin Taymur had been educated at Mayo College, the 'Eton of India'. He too had to sign the non-alienation bond, as well as the letter promising to rely on Britain for help and advice.

When Said bin Taymur was overthrown by his son in 1970, he was generally described as a reactionary despot, a miser and a misanthrope. Peterson's authoritative study presents a more human portrait of the Sultan.[2] It shows how, for example, he was driven in the early years of his reign by the desire to free his country of Britain's control over its internal affairs; to do this, and because he could not find the means to generate income in the coastal areas he controlled, he cut public spending very drastically, inevitably causing stagnation. But he succeeded in his main objective.

An opportunity to replenish Oman's depleted coffers arose in the 1930s with the arrival of an oil company in search of a concession. Sultan Said bin Taymur awarded a preliminary oil concession to a subsidiary of the Iraq Petroleum Company in 1937, but the geologists could not enter the concessionary area since the Sultan did not control it. The concession, however, provided him with enough money to be able to court the tribes of the interior, and by the 1940s he had started to wield some influence over them.

When the Imam of Oman died in 1954, Said bin Taymur seized the opportunity to re-assert Al bu Said authority throughout Oman. A combination of events – the election of a pro-Saudi successor and the arrival to the interior of the oil company's exploratory team – prompted the Sultan to mount a military expedition with British help. In a short time, his forces had occupied all the principal towns of Oman and were successful in uniting the whole country for the first time in a hundred years.

The defeated Imam abdicated, but his brother refused to accept the situation. He appealed to Saudi Arabia for help, aware that King Saud was still chafing at Britain's role in the Buraimi crisis.

Saudi Arabia provided him with military and financial aid and he organized the Oman Liberation Army. In 1957, he led it into Oman. The Sultan, desperate to maintain the new unity of Oman, appealed to Britain for further assistance. In so doing, he lost sight of his earlier objective to make Oman independent. British ground forces, supported by the Royal Air Force (RAF) went into action, and in early 1959, the Oman Liberation Army was defeated.

In the course of providing the Sultan with military aid, the British government reached an agreement with him in 1958; he undertook to extend the wartime lease of the RAF on Masirah island; and in exchange, he would receive substantial British help to establish a national defence force. The Sultan had become even more dependent on Britain.

The Oman Liberation Movement received widespread sympathy and support in the Arab world, where common cause was made with its objectives to overcome the combined powers of an archaic monarch and his colonial supporters. But despite two votes in its favour at the United Nations General Assembly, the Movement came to nothing. It was the Dhufar Revolution, also anti-Sultan and anti-British, which ultimately brought the downfall of Said bin Taymur.

In the meantime, having reunited the Imamate with the Sultanate, Sultan Said left the capital, Muscat, in 1958. He settled in the southern coastal town of Salala in the province of Dhufar where he owned extensive private properties. There he ruled in a highly personal manner which grew increasingly autocratic and anachronistic; he placed so many petty restrictions on the people of Dhufar that many moved to other Gulf states to escape the oppression.

By 1965, a revolution against Said had started in Dhufar. What began as a rebellion against the Sultan's archaic method of rule later developed into a guerrilla war led by the Popular Front for the Liberation of the Occupied Arab Gulf (PFLOAG). Its principal objective was to liberate the Gulf region from both imperialism and from oligarchic rule, and in this it was supported by the neighbouring People's Democratic Republic of Yemen (PDR of Yemen).

Because PFLOAG was a direct threat to its oil and strategic interests, Britain became actively engaged in suppressing it; this involved the mobilization of contingents from the RAF and the

Special Air Service (SAS). In the meantime, Tariq bin Taymur, brother of the Sultan, gave up waiting for him to modernize his administration; despairing of the future at home, he went into voluntary exile. The Sultan had by now become a recluse, so remote a figure that even Qaboos, his son and heir, saw him only on rare occasions. The pressures for change became overwhelming, for time seemed to have stood still in Oman: in Muscat, for example, people had to walk by lantern light, and the gates to the town were closed a few hours after sunset. There were only three schools in the entire country and 10 kilometres (around 6 miles) of paved roads.

By 1970, with British withdrawal from the Gulf only a year away, and with the fighting in Dhufar expanding in scale, Qaboos began to plan a coup. After being educated in Britain, he returned home to live in Salala, where he had grown impatient with his father's antiquated administration. On 23 July 1970, with British approval, his men stormed the Sultan's palace and forced the old man, who had been wounded when trying to resist, to abdicate. He died in exile in London two years later.

Oil in commercial quantities had been discovered in 1964. Although Said bin Taymur had initiated a cautious plan to develop the country with the income from sales, his successor was much more vigorous in his approach. He moved to Muscat, and from there started the process of transforming the capital into a modern city. Schools, houses and hospitals were constructed; public utilities were made available; and development plans were initiated. Government machinery was created to administer the new Oman: a cabinet was formed with ministers of defence, foreign affairs, information, interior, petroleum and minerals, etc. Sultan Qaboos, however, centralized power in his own hands, and made no attempt to introduce any form of participation in government.

The revolution in Dhufar continued. It had by now become the focal point for all political movements in the Arabian peninsula – including the Gulf states – which sought a radical change in the *status quo*: it aimed to bring about the termination of the British role and of monarchical rule; it also sought the introduction of an equitable distribution of the vast oil revenues. Aside from the support of the PDR of Yemen, it also received aid from Iraq, which had refused to establish diplomatic links with Oman after Sultan Qaboos had come to power. Help was also provided by Cuba, China and the USSR.

As his father had done before him, Sultan Qaboos relied increasingly on British military aid and personnel for protection. This enabled him to intensify military operations against the revolutionaries. Around 680 British officers – including some on contract to the Sultan and others from the SAS and RAF – fought on behalf of the Sultan. Two other monarchies provided the same kind of assistance – Iran and Jordan. The presence of Iranian troops in an Arab country angered many at this time and drove a wedge between the new ruler of Oman and his counterparts elsewhere in the Arab world.

The collapse of the Dhufar Revolution at the end of 1975 has been attributed to a number of factors. The combined presence of the British, Jordanian and Iranian military contingents was a major contribution. So too was the scale of Oman's oil revenues after 1973 which provided the Sultan with numerous advantages: he was able to spend lavishly on upgrading his defence forces; and he was able to provide the province of Dhufar with many social and economic reforms, thus tackling the original reasons for the Revolution. Moreover, he granted an amnesty for all Dhufaris who surrendered, and appointed some to senior positions in government. The 1975 Algiers accord between Iraq and Iran also contributed to the collapse of the Revolution, for after it was signed, Iraq discontinued aid to Dhufar. Shortly afterwards, Iraq and Oman established diplomatic relations for the first time.

One of the exiles from the old Sultan's days was his brother, Tariq bin Taymur. When Qaboos assumed power, his uncle returned to Muscat and became Prime Minister. But it soon became clear that nephew and uncle did not agree on the manner in which the country should be governed. Qaboos retained executive and administrative powers, and had no intention of relinquishing them; Tariq disapproved and resigned. But Qaboos's other uncles remained in government: Fahr bin Taymur as Deputy Prime Minister for Security and Defence; and Shabib bin Taymur as Minister of the Environment and Water Resources. The Sultan's second cousin (nephew of Sultan Taymur), Faisal bin Ali, is Minister of National Heritage and Culture; and another nephew of Sultan Taymur, Thuwaini bin Shihab, is the Personal Representative of Qaboos in the cabinet.

In 1981, a state consultative council was established with fifty-five members. It is a purely consultative body whose functions are to recommend amendments to social and economic laws; to recommend solutions to problems; and, when asked by the Sultan, to give him its collective opinion on any subject. Sultan Qaboos has thus provided Oman with all the accoutrements of a modern state, while effectively retaining all the powers his father had.

In his foreign policy, Sultan Qaboos has committed Oman to a course which has at times set it apart from its neighbours and the rest of the Arab world; here again, he has followed in his father's footsteps.

When in 1979 Egypt signed the Camp David agreement with Israel under American auspices, all Arab countries severed diplomatic relations with Egypt – with the exception of Oman and Morocco. The following year, Oman entered into a military agreement with the USA which provides it with air and naval facilities in Oman.

Since the beginning of the Iran–Iraq war, Sultan Qaboos has been very careful to balance his policy towards these countries: conscious of the proximity of Iran – a mere 40 kilometres (25 miles) away – he has refused to endorse the staunch pro-Iraq stand of Kuwait and Saudi Arabia, at the same time joining them in the declarations made by the Gulf Cooperation Council (GCC) on the war itself. Oman broke with tradition in another way in 1985 when it became the second Gulf state (after Kuwait) to establish diplomatic ties with the USSR.

Notes

1 The complete text of a version of the letter is available in J. E. Peterson, *Oman in the Twentieth Century* (London, 1978), p. 224.
2 Ibid.

9 Saudi Arabia, the Powerful Neighbour

Until independence, Britain controlled and administered all international affairs; the Gulf states did not therefore develop the relevant institutions, formal and informal, to handle them on their own. Britain's departure thus left them at a significant disadvantage as to the conduct of their foreign affairs.

The institutions they have since established to deal with external affairs are youthful. Moreover, because they were founded with the help of expatriates, it has taken some time for them to adjust to the specific needs and demands of the Gulf states. During the 1980s, moreover, these states have become particularly vulnerable to external forces, and their institutions are being extended to cope with these pressures. On the one hand, their tiny populations and technological dependence on expatriates have contributed to this vulnerability; on the other, their extensive resources have attracted great international interest.

Because of the enormous power it wields, Saudi Arabia has gradually become the most influential neighbour of the Gulf states. This influence has been growing steadily over the years and became much more marked after the start of the Iraq–Iran war. In fact, it can be said that the security of the Gulf states relies overwhelmingly on that of Saudi Arabia; the two have become inextricably linked.

Since the Kingdom of Saudi Arabia was established in 1932, the various Political Residents and Agents repeatedly acknowledged that it was Britain's natural successor in the Gulf states. The fact that these states had the same language, religion and social order as Saudi Arabia strengthened the likelihood that, were it not for the British presence, Saudi rule would have embraced them as well. Saudi Arabia encompasses more than three-quarters of the Arabian peninsula and as such occupies an area larger than that of the British Isles, France, Benelux, West Germany and Spain combined. It straddles two strategically important bodies of water – the Red Sea and the Gulf – and it has highly diversified geographical features: from the mountains of Asir in the west to the desert of the Rub al-Khali (the Empty Quarter) in the south. It also contains the two holiest shrines of Islam, the mosques of Mecca and Medina, to which pilgrims come from all over the world. It is known, too, to have the world's largest petroleum reserves.

Although it is sparsely populated – estimates range between 6 and 10 million – it is still far ahead of all the Gulf states combined. Its eastern borders run into Kuwait, Qatar, the UAE and Oman; and the causeway completed in 1986 connecting Bahrain with the Saudi mainland has changed Bahrain's island status. Equally important, Saudi Arabia and the Gulf states are ruled by kings, amirs, and sultans; the monarchical principle of hereditary rule prevails. This has bound them together and given them all a 'conservative' outlook. The ruling dynasties in Iraq and Iran, by contrast, were swept away by revolution.

Phase 1: 1913–32

The relationship of the Gulf states with Saudi Arabia has evolved in a number of distinct phases. The first can be said to have started in 1913 when the Wahhabis conquered Hasa (the fertile area on the Gulf coast stretching between Kuwait and Qatar), thus extending their authority to the eastern coast of Arabia. Britain, anxious to maintain its sphere of influence, entered into an agreement shortly afterwards with Abdel Aziz ibn Turki Al Faisal Al Saud (known in the West as Ibn Saud). In it, he undertook to abstain from aggression against or interference with the Gulf states; in exchange, Britain recognized his independence and undertook to protect him from foreign aggression.

During the next decade, Ibn Saud organized the *Ikhwan* (brotherhood), a para-military Wahhabi bedouin movement which was the backbone of his military force, to extend his power throughout the Arabian peninsula. His forward policy reaped him great territorial awards. The climax came in 1924 when Mecca surrendered to his forces; this was followed the next year by the total collapse of the Hashemite dynasty in the Hijaz when Medina and Jeddah fell to the Saudis. In 1926, Ibn Saud was proclaimed King Abdel Aziz of the Hijaz; and in 1932, he established the new Kingdom of Saudi Arabia.

Throughout the period of his expansion, and following the establishment of his kingdom, Ibn Saud had little direct contact with the Gulf states, particularly in view of his great territorial advancement elsewhere. From the beginning of his career, he recognized the value of an alliance with Britain and showed a marked interest in maintaining its friendship. This was based on pragmatic considerations, for one of his greatest assets was his ability to perceive the limitations of his own power, especially in the face of British opposition.

His influence was extremely powerful, however, and extended to all the Gulf states. During this first phase of the relationship, it was felt in different ways in different places. Kuwait was the only Gulf state with which his borders had been officially delineated at an early stage; this took place at a British-sponsored conference held at Ujair (in Hasa) in 1922 when two-thirds of the land claimed by Kuwait was given to Ibn Saud. Shaikh Ahmad al-Jabir of Kuwait was deeply angered by the loss of so much of Kuwaiti territory; he found it particularly difficult to accept when he remembered that, as a young boy in exile, Ibn Saud had taken refuge in Kuwait and he and his family had been treated with great hospitality and respect.

The tension between the two states grew more acute throughout the 1920s. Saudi Arabia did not in those early days have a port of any value in the Gulf; it had to rely instead on those of Kuwait and Bahrain. Ibn Saud wanted to establish his own customs house in Kuwait since it would have been impossible for his officers to collect customs dues along the desert border which separated the two states. Shaikh Ahmad of Kuwait categorically refused Ibn Saud's request, which would have meant that goods in transit for Saudi Arabia would pass through Kuwait free of duty. Ibn Saud retaliated by imposing an economic embargo on Kuwait. The results were disastrous, particularly after the collapse of the pearling industry, when Kuwait relied almost entirely on trade; its consequent decline as an entrepôt for the mainland was dramatic, and this situation lasted for many years.

In Qatar, the Trucial states and Oman, Wahhabi pressure was more subtle. Ibn Saud knew exactly how to gauge the divisions existing within these societies and how to exploit them. His power in Qatar, for example, was extended by supporting the opposition to the ruler there. Unable to defend himself against internal dissension, Shaikh Abdallah of Qatar finally submitted and paid Ibn Saud a secret subsidy as a symbol of deference.

Qatar, Oman and most of the Trucial states had common borders with Saudi Arabia. The exact delineation of these borders did not become an important issue until the oil companies began their exploratory work. In 1930, the Political Resident complained that although Britain held the 'front door' (i.e. the sea coast) of these states, it had no control over the 'back door' (i.e. the inland portions). It was precisely through this back door that Ibn Saud was able to increase his influence. For it was there that the extent of the rulers' jurisdiction was determined, and it was there, away from direct British influence, that Wahhabi power was most acutely felt. The technique used by the Wahhabis to control the tribes was the enforcement of subsidies; this was later to become important when the formal delimiting of Saudi Arabia's borders with these states began.

Phase 2: 1932–58

The second phase in the relationship began in 1932 when the Kingdom of Saudi Arabia was established. Ibn Saud had grown considerably in international stature; and his position both in the Arabian peninsula and *vis-à-vis* the British was secure and appeared to be lasting. In 1933, he signed an oil concession with the American company, Standard Oil Company of California (SoCal), which was the first step to great wealth as well as to a close association with the USA.

Three new developments in the late 1930s caused the King to change his attitude towards Kuwait and Bahrain. The first was the growing interest of Iraq in Kuwait, and of Iran in Bahrain; the second was the discovery of oil, first in Bahrain, and then later in Kuwait; and the third was the 1938 reform movements in both Gulf states.

Ibn Saud's strong rivalry with the Hashemite dynasty of Iraq, who had been his enemies when they had ruled the Hijaz, reinforced his fear that Iraq was attempting to extend its influence to the Gulf. His earlier hostility towards Shaikh Ahmad of Kuwait was replaced by sympathy for a fellow ruler; and a fellow ruler whose power was being eroded by internal opposition when the *majlis* of 1938 was established. Likewise, the persistent Iranian claims to Bahrain were acting to de-stabilize the region, and led the Saudis to support Bahrain; and in so doing, relations with Iran became strained, with little love lost on either side.

Ibn Saud's attitude to the rulers of Kuwait and Bahrain changed perceptibly at this time. He began to show them a new respect. He acknowledged the fact that both men were distantly related to him (through the Anaiza tribal confederation). Both rulers moreover had been challenged in 1938 by a group of their own subjects, a challenge of which Ibn Saud the monarch strongly disapproved. Both had become increasingly independent of their respective subjects for the generation of their income after the discovery of oil, and this placed them in a rank the King considered to be similar to his own. He had by now outgrown his former dependence on Kuwait and Bahrain, and felt confident that they acknowledged his superior rank. So he went on a state visit to Kuwait, the first since he had become King; he was accompanied by a large retinue who placed substantial orders for goods with Kuwaiti merchants. The embargo was officially over and was replaced by a trade agreement. Likewise, the King made a public display of his friendship with the ruler of Bahrain: he sent his oldest son there first, and then followed him in great splendour to the islands.

By contrast, Ibn Saud's relationship with the remaining Gulf states grew more turbulent during this second phase. One reason was that he regarded the tribal origins of their rulers as being remote and not of his own noble blood-line. Another reason concerned the activities of SoCal which wanted to know the exact extent of its concessionary area. The Saudi oil concession ultimately involved both the US and British governments in long discussions and deliberations over the delineation of boundaries. Saudi Arabia claimed territory which the British government, acting on behalf of the Gulf states, refused to accept. The tensions over this issue, which had been building up for some time, finally erupted in early 1949.

SoCal exploratory parties, acting on behalf of Saudi oil interests, began field work in some of the disputed areas. The British government protested, saying that that particular area belonged to Abu Dhabi. Although attempts to solve the crisis through diplomatic channels were made, the Saudi government remained firm about its claims to the disputed area. In 1952, it sent an armed force to one of the villages of Buraimi, an inland oasis claimed by both Abu Dhabi and Oman. This was the start of a particularly long and bitter dispute which became known as the Buraimi crisis.

The arrival of British armed forces having resulted in a military stalemate, it was agreed that still more negotiations would take place; and that for their duration, all military action in Buraimi would cease. Both sides – Britain acting on behalf of Abu Dhabi and Oman on one side, and Saudi Arabia on the other – therefore presented written testimonies to an international tribunal; they detailed, as a basis for decision, tribal loyalties (past and present) and their influence on the jurisdiction of Buraimi. But in the wake of dramatic mutual accusations by the two sides, the proceedings broke down. Military action was resumed in late 1955, when British forces forcibly evicted the Saudi contingent still based in the oasis. The British government then 'awarded' three of the villages in Buraimi to Oman, and the remaining four to Abu Dhabi.

That part of the oasis given to Abu Dhabi is today called al-Ain (after one of the principal villages) and constitutes an important part of the UAE; it is especially significant as the oasis of which Shaikh Zayid, President of the UAE, was formerly the governor. It has been developed into a beautiful inland retreat; old buildings have been restored and gardens carefully tended; it is also the site of the University of al-Ain, the only university in the UAE, and there are plans to build an international airport there.

Saudi Arabia refused formally to acknowledge the rights of Abu Dhabi and Oman in Buraimi (al-Ain); and its boundary with the other states was not to be fully accepted for over two decades. This put a significant strain on relations between Saudi Arabia and Abu Dhabi which persisted even after the establishment of the UAE; Saudi Arabia was angered both by the loss of Buraimi and by Britain's role. As a result, Saudi Arabia withheld diplomatic recognition of the UAE in 1971. It was not until 1974 that an agreement was reached with Shaikh Zayid, Amir of Abu Dhabi and President of the UAE: in it, Saudi Arabia obtained a corridor to the sea through Abu Dhabi; in return, Saudi Arabia recognized al-Ain as belonging to Abu Dhabi. Saudi diplomatic relations with the UAE were then established.

In the meantime, Saudi Arabia was well on the way to becoming acknowledged as one of the most potentially wealthy nations of the world. It was also being regarded as an important country in the Arab world, and its representatives were diplomatically accredited to all the major nations, with the exception of the USSR. The old King, Ibn Saud, frail and in poor health, was active until the end: in those last years he wished to transform his vast country from a tribal society into a centrally governed state. As the process of modernization began, one factor remained constant: the fundamental law of Saudi Arabia was the strict adherence to the *Shariah*, the sacred law of Islam.

King Abdel Aziz (Ibn Saud) died in November 1953 and was succeeded by his Heir Apparent, Saud ibn Abdel Aziz (1953–64). King Saud's reign was a troubled one, beset internally by the problems of disbursing the huge income from oil in an equitable manner; and externally by the conflicting challenges facing the Arab world. Financial difficulties were particularly marked; there seemed to be little control over the vast monies pouring in from oil sales, and spending soon exceeded income. Deficits in the national budget curtailed the development and expansion of the infrastructures necessary for the establishment of a modern state. Unaccustomed to coping with such matters, King Saud turned his attention instead to foreign affairs, which he felt better equipped to deal with.

He responded enthusiastically to the policies of pan-Arabism enunciated by Gamal Abdel Nasser of Egypt, and in 1955, Saudi Arabia entered into a treaty with Egypt. The King, embittered by his country's recent humiliation in Buraimi, saw in Nasser a natural ally who was determined to resist British influence in the Arab world. He was also keen to join forces with Egypt in curtailing the power of Saudi Arabia's old enemies, the Hashemites, whose dynasties ruled Iraq and Jordan in close British alliance. Nasser regarded the alliance with Saudi Arabia as a significant step towards Arab unity; he was especially grateful for the funds provided by Saudi Arabia which enabled Egypt to continue the process. What was later to be termed by Western journalists as Saudi Arabia's 'cheque-book diplomacy' had started. King Saud did not manifest his friendship and alliance with Egypt by money alone. In November 1956, after a joint Anglo-French and Israeli force attacked Egypt following the nationalization of the Suez Canal, Saudi Arabia severed diplomatic relations with Britain and

France; it also refused to allow Saudi oil to reach those two countries, thus implementing the first Arab oil embargo.

But by 1958, relations between Egypt and Saudi Arabia had cooled considerably. The turning-point probably occurred in late 1957 when King Saud embarked on a state visit – his first – to the USA. The latter country had moved into the forefront of Arab affairs after the decline in power of France and Britain following the Suez fiasco. And one of the earliest manifestations of this was the Eisenhower Doctrine. This policy was announced in early 1957 by President Eisenhower who promised US financial and military aid to any Arab country which required assistance in its fight against communism. The USA was deeply suspicious of the fact that the USSR had come to Egypt's help in constructing the much-needed Aswan Dam, despite having itself refused Nasser's earlier overtures for assistance. It denied the validity of Nasser's policy of 'positive neutrality' and viewed the Aswan Dam as a superpower issue between the USA and the USSR. The politics of the Cold War had reached the Arab world.

The USA wished to make Saudi Arabia, the Arab country with the greatest American interests, the spearhead of the Eisenhower Doctrine. In the meantime, a major shift in inter-Arab alliances was emerging. King Saud led his country away from the close relationship with Egypt. In this, he was motivated by the inherent threat of the Egyptian revolution to monarchical rule and the call of Arab socialism. He was equally worried by the prospects of a Soviet *rapprochement*; as the ruler of a state where religion was integrated into daily life, any kind of an alliance with an atheist government was anathema to him.

Thus he went to the USA on his state visit. The visit itself was marked by two events which symbolize the love–hate relationship between the two countries and which has since become standard. Upon arriving in New York City, his first port of call, he was totally ignored by the Mayor who refused to extend him even the most basic courtesies. He did not greet the visiting King, despite a strong request from Washington to welcome him in the warmest manner possible. The Mayor apparently acted out of deference to the large Jewish population of New York who had accused the King of being anti-Semitic.

So it was through a chillingly hostile and unwelcoming city that King Saud entered the USA on his first state visit. When he arrived in Washington, however, President Eisenhower and his government extended themselves in an effort both to offset the snubs of New York and to convince the King of the importance of the Eisenhower Doctrine, In this they were successful. By the end of the visit, Saudi Arabia had accepted US military and technical assistance to develop a modern army, as well as economic aid for its developmental programmes.

The state visit was an important milestone in Saudi–American relations. It marked the beginning of the strong military and political alliance between the two countries which has continued to grow. Moreover, it moved Saudi Arabia away from the forefront of the 'progressive' states opposed to western influence in the Arab world and placed it firmly in the 'conservative' flank. Symbolic of this change was the state visit of King Saud to Iraq a few months later. Saudi Arabia was now allied to the British-protected states of Iraq and Jordan, and no longer to Egypt and Syria. Inevitably, the third phase in its relations with the Gulf states had started.

Phase 3: 1958–71

Saudi Arabia's attitude and policies towards the Gulf states mellowed considerably in this phase. It was no longer overtly resentful of their British protection. It also realized that its own oil reserves were of such a magnitude that it was not worth while to press for more land from its neighbours. Moreover, it was preoccupied with its own internal problems of development and social change and was noticeably anxious to rationalize its relationship with its neighbours. The most important area of dispute had been the border issues, so Saudi Arabia now attempted to resolve many of these problems.

A significant step in this process occurred in 1958 when Saudi Arabia and Bahrain signed the first continental shelf boundary agreement in the Gulf, whereby the Abu Safa oilfields were given to Saudi Arabia, but the income from them was to be shared equally between the two countries. It is interesting to note that the Abu Safa oilfields have been amongst the most active of Saudi Arabia during the 1980s despite the dramatic cutback in production; this activity was maintained in order to ensure that Bahrain would continue to receive a reasonable oil income. This first continental shelf agreement in the Gulf paved the way for many more: between Iran and Qatar, Bahrain and Iran, Abu Dhabi and Qatar, and Oman and Iran.

In the meantime, the financial and administrative affairs of the Kingdom had reached such a low level that the Al Saud decided that only a dramatic change would solve the internal problems of the state. While the King was abroad on a private visit in 1964, he was replaced by his brother Faisal ibn Abdel Aziz (1964–75) who had had long experience as Foreign Minister.

The mellowing attitude towards the Gulf states begun in 1958 continued. The next step was taken in 1965 when the neutral zone with Kuwait – which had been devised in 1922 by British officials – was partitioned equally between the two states. That same year, Saudi Arabia reached an agreement with Qatar on their common boundary. Only the border issue with Abu Dhabi remained. And here Saudi Arabia refused to compromise, the memory of its eviction from Buraimi still strong; it preferred to wait for the propitious moment to settle this long and outstanding problem.

The defeat of the Egyptian, Syrian and Jordanian armies in the June 1967 Arab–Israeli war brought about major changes in Arab regional politics. Whereas previously Nasser's Egypt had been the undisputed leader of the Arab world, its devastating failure in battle began the decline of its influence. Not only was its army crushed and mangled; its economy was in ruins. At the summit for Arab heads of state which convened shortly afterwards in Khartoum, it fell to Saudi Arabia to take on at least part of the leadership role previously assumed by Egypt. This led to heavy Saudi and Kuwaiti financial subsidies to the states confronting Israel.

In the meantime, a significant change in the Gulf region was about to take place. This was the withdrawal of Britain after a century and a half; its quiet and undramatic replacement by Saudi Arabia ushered in the fourth phase in the relationship with the Gulf states.

Phase 4: 1971–

The power which had dominated Gulf waters for 150 years left the area permanently in 1971. The political structures it had established over this time now became vulnerable to the forces of change. Saudi policy towards the Gulf states adjusted very quickly. This policy transcended the narrow confines of its previous relationships, and was governed by new considerations. With its increased stature, it functioned on two levels: that of its relationship to the entire Gulf region, including Iran and Iraq; and its relationship to the Arab world as a whole.

Saudi Arabia gradually drew its mantle of protection over the small Gulf states, and viewed its relationship with them as part of a wider regional perspective. When, for example, Iraq laid claim in 1973 to the islands of Wakrah and Bubiyan which Kuwait considered as part of its own territory, Saudi Arabia acted to maintain the *status quo*; it quietly (and temporarily) dropped previous claims it had in other islands in Kuwait, and defended Wakrah and Bubiyan against Iraqi moves. Saudi Arabia thus replaced Britain in seeking to consolidate the established territorial order of the region.

In the meantime, the USA was actively seeking the establishment of a new security system to fill the 'power vacuum' resulting from Britain's departure. Its primary motivation was the fear of Soviet encroachment on what – because of its economic importance – had become a region of vital importance to western industrial countries. The Nixon administration therefore formulated what became known as the 'twin pillar' policy: reliance on both Iran and Saudi Arabia.

Of the two, Iran was regarded as militarily more capable of securing western interests. The Shah was accordingly given almost unlimited American military and intelligence assistance, and gradually came to be regarded as the 'policeman of the Gulf'. As military aid of all kinds arrived in astonishing strength from the USA, the ambitions of the Shah grew correspondingly. He was provided, for example, with covert CIA aid to help the Kurdish revolt against the central government in Iraq; this gave him great leverage over Iraq and enabled him in 1975 to impose the Algiers agreement whereby Iraq conceded part of the Shatt al-Arab waterway to Iran. This ultimately became one of the reasons for the Iraq–Iran war.[1] Saudi Arabia, on the other hand, was regarded as the stabilizing influence on the Gulf states; US support therefore enabled it to enhance its position in the Gulf region and throughout the Arab world.

But a new dynamism, which the twin pillar policy had not taken into account, had entered the Arab world. It was registered in a closing of ranks, and extended to all countries, 'progressive' and 'conservative' alike. The 1973 Arab–Israeli war was an important example, and marked the climax of this trend. During the first week of the war, the Arab armies reversed many of the advances Israel had made in 1967, the most important being the crossing of the Bar Lev line in Egypt. The USA came in heavily on the side of Israel and immediately organized a massive airlift of military hardware to Tel Aviv. Refusing to accept this unconditional support of Israel, the Organization of Arab Petroleum Exporting Countries (OAPEC) met in Kuwait and announced a 5 per cent cutback per month in oil production until Israel withdrew from all the Arab land it had occupied. Two days later, and in direct response to the military help they insisted on providing Israel, King Faisal imposed an oil embargo on the USA and Holland. The Gulf states, together with all Arab oil-producing countries, followed suit.

This was the beginning of the Arab oil boycott which lasted for five months and caused a major economic crisis in Western Europe and the USA. The conservation of fuel became an overwhelming priority in the industrial world, where massive projects to develop alternative sources of energy were instigated. In the meantime, industries which had relied on unlimited supplies of cheap oil became unable to continue production; long queues of motorists waiting for petrol became a common sight in Europe; speed limits were imposed everywhere to slow down petrol consumption; drastic measures were taken to cut down on the heating of homes, schools and factories as millions faced the prospect of a cold and dark winter. Desperate for oil, governments and major institutions became prepared to pay much higher prices from those non-Arab countries, like Iran, which had not joined the embargo: prices rose dramatically from $3 to $17 per barrel in a few weeks. During the following eleven years, they continued their upward trend, again increasing dramatically after the fall of the Shah of Iran in 1979.

Although the oil embargo did not succeed in changing US policy towards Israel, it had a number of important repercussions, three of which had a lasting impact. The first was what became known as Arab linkage strategy: the integration of government policy in Saudi Arabia and the Gulf states with events in the northern part of the Arab world. This was a new departure, for hitherto there had been little direct linkage between the two. Although Saudi Arabia had utilized what was later termed its 'oil weapon' against

France and Britain after Suez in 1956, it had carried little weight because Saudi Arabia had acted on its own.

The Gulf states, of course, had been outside the mainstream of the Arab world until independence; this was a direct result of British policy which had carefully sought to maintain that separateness. Although events leading to the establishment of the 1938 reform movement in Kuwait were connected with the Palestine crisis of 1936–9, they were a phenomenon rather than a common occurrence. Once oil was discovered in the Gulf states, Britain became even more reluctant to allow the states to become integrated with the northern Arab world.

The oil embargo occurred in 1973, only two years after Britain had withdrawn from the Gulf; it demonstrated the intrinsic Arab nature of the Gulf states despite 150 years of British attempts to isolate them. Linkage strategy presented the first effective pan-Arab effort to close ranks against the USA and other countries which persisted in aiding Israel. In 1974, at a meeting of the Arab heads of state in Rabat, the Palestine Liberation Organization (PLO) was recognized as the sole legitimate representative of the Palestinian people; the Palestine question for the first time was accorded its central place in regional Arab politics and no longer regarded as being merely a refugee problem. That same year, PLO offices were established throughout the world with full Arab backing.

Arab linkage strategy was also a strong manifestation of the close integration of the Gulf with the northern Arab world despite the substantial differences superimposed by colonial domination. Above all, perhaps, it represented an important step in the process of increased interaction between the Gulf states and the rest of the Arab world which has become more important in recent years. But this has not been without its cost. The visit to Abu Dhabi of the Syrian Foreign Minister in 1977, for example, resulted in the accidental assassination of the Minister of State for Foreign Affairs of the UAE, Dr Sayf bin Ghubbash.

An extraordinary financial windfall accompanied the steep rise in the price of oil. Whereas during the 1960s it had been sold for $2 per barrel, in early 1974 it commanded eight times more and by 1981, the cost was closer to $34. Saudi Arabia and the Gulf states, with their small populations, could hardly cope with the great wealth which was fast accumulating. Not having been prepared for such a massive and sudden economic transformation, they lacked the requisite machinery to handle the new situation. The extent of the new wealth was breathtaking. In an attempt to illustrate its scale, *The Economist* (27 June 1987) estimated that after the 1973–4 price rises, Saudi Arabia and some of its OPEC allies were accumulating foreign-exchange surpluses at around $115,000 a second; and that they could have bought the equivalent of the four British clearing banks every eleven days, or all the equities on the London Stock Exchange after nine months; and that in under thirteen years, they could have supplied every adult Arab with an annuity of $115 per week.

In an effort to disburse the new income in as constructive a manner as possible, Saudi Arabia and the Gulf states began to expand their infrastructural and social services at a rapid pace. Immense projects of all kinds were implemented in the most unlikely places, a large number of which inevitably turned out to be white elephants. These projects required large supplies of manpower to execute, administer and service them on a long-term basis. So considerable contingents of foreigners began to arrive; while at first many were Arabs from Egypt, Sudan, Palestine, Jordan and Lebanon, the trend during the 1980s has been towards recruiting Asians from Korea, the Philippines and Sri Lanka. Within a short time, the citizens of a number of Gulf states were outnumbered by expatriates.

One of the results of the vast wealth enjoyed by Saudi Arabia – and to a lesser extent, the Gulf states – was that the balance of power in the Arab world shifted away from Egypt and moved eastwards. By virtue of its great financial power, Saudi Arabia became the most important Arab country. It became even more so after 1977, when President Sadat of Egypt demonstrated his willingness to make a separate peace treaty with Israel; this was the result of the US Secretary of State, Dr Kissinger's step-by-step diplomacy, which advocated bi-lateral negotiations, thereby eroding the foundations of Arab unity which had been manifested in the oil embargo. With Egypt consequently ostracized, Saudi Arabia was firmly established as the pivotal state in Arab politics.

In early 1975, the elderly and ascetic King Faisal was murdered by his young nephew for reasons never entirely explained. He was succeeded by his brother, Khalid ibn Abdel Aziz (1975–82). King Khalid was an invalid for much of his reign during which the most important decision-maker in the Kingdom was his brother Fahd ibn Abdel Aziz, the Crown Prince. When King Khalid died of heart failure in 1982, he was succeeded by King Fahd.

The beginning of King Fahd's reign coincided with the strengthening and expansion of Saudi Arabia's strategic alliance with the USA. This followed the collapse in 1979 of the Shah's régime in Iran and the establishment of the Islamic Republic under the leadership of the Ayatollah Khomeini. This at one stroke had removed what the USA had come to rely on as Britain's military successor in the Gulf and replaced it with a strongly anti-American government. The outbreak of the Iraq–Iran war the following year posed a threat of enormous proportions to the security of the entire region.

Saudi Arabia turned more openly than before to the USA for arms and military support to withstand these external forces. During 1979, it had experienced two major internal upheavals which undermined the very security of the Kingdom. The first of these was the seizure in November of the Grand Mosque at Mecca under the leadership of Juhayman bin Muhammad bin Sayf al-Utaybi, a member of the large and powerful Utayba tribe. He and his numerous followers were driven by the deep-rooted desire to restore the purity and essence of Islam to Saudi Arabia. Their motive in seizing its holiest shrine by force of arms was to call attention to the religious laxity prevalent in the Kingdom. They regarded the Al Saud, the custodians of the Grand Mosque, as having failed in their duty as Wahhabis to maintain the original mission of the movement. In fact, James Buchan, author of a chapter in the thoughtful book by David Holden and Richard Johns on the Al Saud,[2] saw in Juhayman and his men the modern equivalent of the *Ikhwan* of King Ibn Saud.

They remained in control of the Grand Mosque for two weeks, repelling numerous attempts by the Saudi armed forces to dislodge them. The government was profoundly shaken by the siege, and was thrown into disarray trying to decide how to handle it. News reports were carefully muted, but enough information leaked out to shock the entire Muslim world profoundly, particularly when it was known that scores of people had been injured, and many killed. The siege ended when its leaders finally ran out of ammunition and surrendered; it has also been said that a French anti-terrorist squad planned the final assault on the besiegers, although the Saudi National Guard actually carried it out.

The second upheaval occurred in the rich, oil-producing province of Hasa, on the eastern coast and a few miles away from the Gulf states. Its population is predominantly Shia, and as such has been regarded as the Achilles' heel of the Saudi Kingdom, particularly after the Iranian Revolution. Hasa had been governed for decades by various members of the Ibn Jiluwi family, relatives of the Al Saud, who were renowned for the close control they exercised over the province. This control was deeply resented by the Hasawis (people of Hasa) who were also conscious of having received very little of the enormous wealth of the country compared with their compatriots elsewhere in Saudi Arabia, although they constituted the backbone of the labour force in the oilfields which produced that wealth.

Encouraged by the militant Shiism of Ayatollah Khomeini's republic in Iran as well as by the siege of the Grand Mosque which was just coming to an end, the leaders of the Shia community announced that they would be marching in public during *Ashura* (the Shia day of commemoration of its martyrs), in open defiance of a long-standing law banning any public demonstrations on that day. When a policeman struck a demonstrator, there was almost immediate reaction. Crowds thronged the streets in the city of Qatif, setting fire to cars, breaking into shops and looting. When calm was finally restored, the cost in human lives was found to have been high: seventeen people had been killed by the security forces and many were wounded.[3]

Both events caused a deep crisis in the Saudi government. The seizure of the Grand Mosque undermined its essential role as custodian of the holiest shrine of Islam, and at the same time questioned the legitimacy of the Al Saud. The Shia riots brought home the vulnerability of the oil-producing province and raised the possibility of its people – who had so many resentments against Saudi rule – turning to Iran for guidance and leadership.

In an attempt to heal the obvious breach with the Hasawis, the government began to earmark large sums of money towards developmental projects there to improve housing, health and education. It also removed the Ibn Jaluwi governor of the province, and replaced him with the son of King Fahd, Prince Muhammad ibn Fahd, who immediately set about trying to improve relations. In another effort to restore general confidence, the government announced that the King had authorized the setting-up of a consultative council which would provide the first formal attempts at participation. To date, however, this council has not been formed, but other measures to counteract the accusations of Juhayman have been implemented: they concern an insistence on rules and regulations which comply with strict Islamic laws and principles.

But despite these and other concessions, the government remained concerned. It relied more than ever on the US for support in the problems it had faced in 1979. In return, it became an established instrument for the implementation of US foreign policy in the Arab world and elsewhere. It opposed a proposal by Arab states to impose an embargo on Egypt (and the USA), for example, in 1979 after the Camp David Agreement between Egypt and Israel was signed. In 1981, it funded Jordanian purchases of US arms in order to prevent Jordan from turning to the USSR. More recently, the 'Irangate' disclosures have revealed that Saudi Arabia secretly supplied the Reagan administration with $32 million for the Nicaraguan Contras in order to bypass Congressional restrictions. And that in 1981, a quiet agreement was made: in return for providing the Reagan administration with money with which to help rebel forces in Angola (again because of Congressional restrictions), Saudi Arabia would receive the full support of the administration to persuade Congress to sell it the Airborne Warning and Control System Aircraft (AWACS) it needed for its own defence.[4]

The love–hate relationship which had marked King Saud's state visit in 1957 has survived into the 1980s: the powerful Zionist lobby had agitated against the sale of the AWACS despite the diplomatic and financial support Saudi Arabia has given the USA over the past decade and a half. Moreover, the US government has continued to rely to a great extent on Saudi Arabia to provide the Gulf states – which supply the western industrial countries with a large proportion of their oil – with strategic stability.

The Gulf states are at present firmly within the Saudi sphere of influence. This continues a trend set by Saudi Arabia after the British withdrawal in 1971 which has gained in strength as conditions in the region have evolved. The Saudis basically play a security role that is manifested in different ways and to different degrees in the various states.

Militarily, all the states except Kuwait have bi-lateral mutual security pacts with Saudi Arabia. The first was signed by Bahrain following the discovery of the attempted coup there in 1981.

Acutely conscious of its inability to defend itself in the face of the growing climate of militancy in the region, Bahrain turned to Saudi Arabia. Within a short time, all the other states had followed suit. Only Kuwait has not signed such an agreement, tenaciously asserting its ability to defend itself. Its pride in its considerable educational, cultural and political achievements and its strong feelings of independence have been expressed in its desire to remain aloof from such an undertaking. It is noteworthy that Kuwait acted on its own when it decided in 1987 to approach the superpowers to re-flag its tankers.

Until 1985, Kuwait was also the only Gulf state which had established diplomatic relations with the USSR. Saudi Arabia had led the other states in this, and has refused since the end of World War II to exchange representatives with that country. In 1985, both Oman and the UAE altered the situation by joining Kuwait; they both established diplomatic ties with the USSR. Qatar followed suit in 1988.

Saudi influence has also been extended on the financial and economic levels. Bahrain's oil revenues are low and depend entirely on the Abu Safa offshore fields which it shares with Saudi Arabia. The rest of its income is earned through its dry dock, its aluminium smelter, and its various banking services, commercial and transport sectors. Many of these are linked to Saudi Arabia, either directly or through Saudi influence in the Gulf Cooperation Council (GCC). Moreover, Bahrain receives direct financial aid from Saudi Arabia. Qatar, which is very wealthy from its oil revenues, receives economic support from Saudi Arabia: one example is the integration of the Qatari iron and steel industry into Saudi development projects. And Oman is the recipient of direct financial aid from Saudi Arabia.

Politically, Saudi Arabia has advocated strong conservative policies in the Gulf states. These have ranged from the banning of alcohol in keeping with Islamic principles to the strengthening of government control in internal affairs. It has been said, for example, that it was Saudi pressure which finally caused the Amir of Bahrain to dissolve the National Assembly in 1975. Once again, only Kuwait remained aloof from these influences; it continued to pride itself on its free press and democratic form of government until 1986, and even then made it clear that the reasons for the changes were internal.

As the most important oil producer, Saudi Arabia has set the parameters for the oil policies of the Gulf states. By and large, they have become joint policies with those of Saudi Arabia, although on occasion one or more of the states displayed a marked reluctance to accept them. In 1982–3, for example, the UAE voiced its objection to the price cuts and production quotas; the Oil Minister at first publicly refused to lower the price of UAE crude oil and only accepted the slowdown in production after the direct intervention of King Fahd who sent an emissary to Shaikh Zayid, the President of the UAE, to convince him of the importance of doing so.

There can be little doubt that Saudi Arabia has become the successor to Britain *vis-à-vis* the Gulf states. Although these states have systematically set out to acquire modern standing armies and defence systems, their reliance on expatriate manpower in both junior and senior positions has weakened their ability to defend themselves. Their security has become linked to that of their powerful neighbour: and so their future has become intertwined with that of Saudi Arabia.

Notes

1   Anthony H. Cordesman, *The Gulf and the Search for Strategic Stability* (Colorado, 1984), p. 57.
2   'The return of the Ikhwan', in David Holden and Richard Johns, *The House of Saud* (London, 1981), ch. 25.
3   Ibid., ch. 25.
4   *The Guardian*, 6 July 1987.

10   The International Setting

The Gulf Cooperation Council

In February 1981, a few months after the war between Iraq and Iran had started, the Foreign Ministers of the five Gulf states and Saudi Arabia held a meeting in Riyadh. They had come together in direct response to the new challenges threatening the region, to seek a collective course of action. Before the meeting was over, they had decided to form a regional political grouping, the Gulf Cooperation Council (GCC). Its official inauguration took place in May 1981 when the six heads of states met in Abu Dhabi. Security was the main stimulus of the new organization, but its declared objective was to effect the social and economic integration of the member states.

The GCC is made up of three bodies. The highest authority is the Supreme Council which consists of the six heads of state and holds one regular session every year. The chairmanship of the Supreme Council is passed in alphabetical order to each of the heads of state, and each member has one vote. Directly attached to the Supreme Council is the Commission for the Settlement of Disputes (between member states). Second is the Ministerial Council which is made up of the six Foreign Ministers or other delegated Ministers. It holds four regular sessions a year. The third body is the General Secretariat based in Riyadh, the headquarters of the GCC. Dr Abdulla Bishara, who has been the Secretary General since the establishment of the GCC, is a Kuwaiti who had served as his country's representative at the United Nations. There are two Assistant Secretaries General: Ibrahim Subhi, an Omani, in charge of political affairs; and Dr Abdallah El-Kuwaiz, a Saudi, in charge of economic affairs.

Early forms of regional cooperation

The movement towards cooperation between the Gulf states and Saudi Arabia had been gathering momentum during the 1970s. It had only become possible, of course, once the Gulf states were fully independent to conduct their foreign relations, which did not happen until after Britain's departure in 1971. The pattern for the new order was set by Kuwait, which had attained independence in 1961 and was anxious to establish links with the young states. A series of bi-lateral agreements were signed which put into practice the concept of cooperation in economic and social affairs. Kuwait signed one such agreement with the UAE in 1971, and another with Bahrain the next year. Other countries followed suit during those early years. These bi-lateral agreements went a long way to removing economic and social barriers between the states; the exemption of customs duty, the exchange of expertise, and the establishment of joint ventures were some of the results.

At the same time, there was a more generalized movement to bring together the Gulf states and the regional powers, Iraq and Saudi Arabia – all Arab countries – in as many ways as possible. During the latter part of the 1970s, this took the form of meetings between specific government ministries: of education, of trade and industry, of health, etc. The objective was to correlate and coordinate their respective work and interests as much as possible.

A significant outcome of these meetings was the creation of a number of institutions designed to create strong links between the countries. For example, the meetings of the ministries of education resulted in the formation of the Gulf University, which is based in Bahrain; it is run jointly by the Gulf states, Saudi Arabia and Iraq. Another institution created during this period was the Gulf Organization for Industrial Consultancy based in Qatar; it is a consultative body whose main function is to promote the cooperation and coordination of the member countries in chemical, petrochemical and other industrial projects. The Gulf Ports Union was also established on behalf of the same countries.

Not all the institutions created at this time grouped together the same seven countries. For example, the shareholders of the United Arab Shipping Company are Bahrain, Qatar, Kuwait, the UAE, Iraq and Saudi Arabia; Oman did not join. Gulf Air, the airline company, does not include Iraq, Kuwait or Saudi Arabia, all of which have their own national airlines.

By the end of the 1970s, the links between the Gulf states had grown substantially. The many meetings which took place to design, establish and administer institutions inevitably forged close personal relationships between the delegates. They also promoted a knowledge and experience of neighbouring states and societies hitherto restricted by the binding nature of British treaty relations. Travel to and from the Gulf states by their respective citizens increased dramatically, and a strong sense of common identity emerged.

Since most of the Gulf states were still in the process of developing their infrastructures, it was natural for them to seek a coordination of effort. Although Kuwait – like Iraq, and to a lesser extent, Saudi Arabia – was more advanced than the others, it actively promoted cooperation as the means to bring about some sort of unity to the region. In the early developmental phases of the Gulf states, a duplication of many projects had resulted. Far too many international airports were built immediately after independence, for example; the existence of one in Sharjah and another just a few miles away in Dubai revealed a crying need for coordinated planning. After their income from oil quadrupled in 1974, many states sought to diversify their economies by turning to industry. The extraordinarily small size of an individual state's market, the lack of local expertise, the reliance on expatriate manpower and other such limitations made it imperative for them to seek rational alternatives.

Collective security

Security and defence remained outside the scope of the many meetings and outside the policy-coordinating bodies established at this time. A certain uneasiness prevailed, based on the growing strength of Iran, which had full US backing; the Gulf states were hesitant about being linked either with or against it.

In late 1976, Sultan Qaboos of Oman took the initiative and organized a meeting in Muscat for the Foreign Ministers of all the littoral states in the Gulf; this included the five Gulf states and the three regional powers, Iraq, Iran and Saudi Arabia. The objective of the meeting was to seek a coordinated regional security and defence policy. But in view of the many differences between them, it was inevitable perhaps that they were unable to agree on a common position.

That same year, the Saudi Minister of the Interior, Prince Naif, visited each of the five Gulf states. His objective was to integrate all information with a bearing on internal security; the collection of this form of information is usually the work of the ministries of the interior. After consulting his counterparts in the five states, he established working links with their respective institutions to create an effective means of sharing intelligence information. Moreover, the six countries agreed to work together to maintain internal security from then on. As relations between the different ministries of the interior strengthened as a result of Prince Naif's initiative, so too did their cooperation.[1]

When the member states of the GCC came together in 1981, therefore, the groundwork for their new organization had in effect already been prepared. The GCC was ready for more widespread measures to strengthen and promote closer relations. Shortly after its inauguration, studies were prepared to coordinate defence policies and to cooperate in joint exercises. The majority of the member states were keen to avoid encouraging superpower rivalry in the Gulf; they made it clear that the GCC intended to provide for its own protection rather than rely on outside help. Only Oman stood aloof from these policy decisions. It had already entered into a military agreement with the USA in 1980, and it was one of only two Arab countries – Morocco was the other – which had accepted the Camp David Agreements between Israel and Egypt.

Despite such differences in outlook, the GCC announced in 1983 that it was setting up a rapid deployment force, and shortly after, this force undertook military exercises in Gulf waters. The theme of military self-reliance was pronounced on behalf of the GCC by Abdulla Bishara, the charismatic Secretary General, in a magazine interview in 1983: Gulf security had to be provided by the people of the Gulf; foreign troops, no matter how friendly, could never act in the interests of the Gulf.[2] The next year, the GCC announced that it had decided to create a 'strike force' under the command of a Saudi general. As the war between Iraq and Iran progressed and took on new and dangerous dimensions, however, the GCC has referred less and less to the themes of military self-sufficiency and self-reliance; the focus has been rather on deterrence, and the non-military means of bringing it about.

Economic integration

The GCC has made considerable progress towards attaining its
objectives of economic integration. The quiet establishment of a
common market within the member states has been proceeding
at a steady and uninterrupted pace. Common regulations in many
different areas have been introduced throughout the member
states; they have resulted in standardized procedure in a wide
range of commercial, cultural and social endeavours. Moreover,
a number of decisions have been taken to strengthen economic
and commercial collaboration between the six states: customs
duties on domestically produced goods have been removed; only
a low tariff on imported foreign goods exists; and goods passing
in transit from one GCC country to another are exempt from
dues or taxes.

Citizens of GCC states are accorded many privileges. They are
treated as nationals in many cases, and do not require work
permits. They are not subject to the restrictions on investments
which bind foreigners, and are even entitled to own a limited
amount of residential property. Travel to and from other GCC
countries is also more free than it is for foreigners.

In 1982, the GCC established the Gulf Investment Corporation
as part of its efforts to coordinate the economies of the member
states. It began operations three years later, and has a paid-up
capital of around $540 million. A significant part of its investments
has been in projects in the GCC states, particularly since the
recession caused by declining oil revenues. It has interests in a
dairy project in Qatar, a pharmaceutical company in Kuwait, a
titanium dioxide plant in Saudi Arabia (for the production of
pigment for plastics and textiles), a foil mill in Bahrain and a bio-
engineering chicken-breeding project in Saudi Arabia.

One of the items of discussion at future GCC meetings will be
the possibility of aligning the currencies of the member states.
This would entail the coordination of exchange rates, and the
ultimate free flow of trade and capital between them. Another
objective of the GCC is to work towards a currency union.

The economic links between the member states have grown
considerably. They have created a much bigger market than had
existed before 1981. This is mostly due to the Saudi share, which
is so much larger than that of all the other states combined. The
total population (including expatriates) of the five Gulf states

alone is around 4 million; that of the GCC, which includes Saudi Arabia, is much more significant at around 14 million. Because of its large size and overwhelming economic power, Saudi Arabia is inevitably the dominant power within the GCC. It could be said, moreover, that the GCC has provided Saudi Arabia with the institutional structure to exercise its influence.

Saudi influence

This was illustrated during the 1986 crisis between Qatar and Bahrain over the Hawar islands. It was basically a territorial dispute whose roots went back to the 1930s when the Zubarah issue was at its height. The Political Resident of that time was horrified when a new conflict arose between the two states over these islands which lie 3 kilometres (just under 2 miles) off the west coast of Qatar; he could not face a repeat performance of what he regarded as the 'eternal' Zubarah problem. He therefore called on both Qatar and Bahrain to present written proof of ownership.

Bahrain, with the help of Belgrave, the British adviser, prepared lengthy documents. But Qatar protested against these methods; the ruler maintained that Hawar belonged to him and everyone knew it; moreover, he lacked the expertise to put together a legal portfolio. The Political Resident therefore 'awarded' the islands to Bahrain in 1939. His successor, however, questioned the hasty award. He feared it would only lead to further disputes between the two states, particularly since the islands have various rocks, islets, reefs and shoal waters, some of which are very close to the Qatari coast. Qatar has consistently refused to accept the finality of the award, which had been made without due consideration of its case for ownership. Since the islands are largely uninhabited, however, an uneasy calm has prevailed there over the years and little has been done to exercise jurisdiction.

In March 1982, the government of Qatar strongly protested when Bahrain named a naval vessel *The Hawar*. Qatar viewed this as provocative, claiming again that the islands were within Qatar's territorial waters. A few days later, the GCC held a meeting at which it attempted to resolve the crisis in an amicable manner. Both Qatar and Bahrain agreed to freeze the situation and avoid taking any measures which would exacerbate the dispute.

But four years later, on 26 April 1986, the Hawar islands caused another crisis between Qatar and Bahrain. A station for Bahraini coastguards was being constructed on Fasht al-Dibal, one of the islets belonging to Hawar; it is a rocky and small place, barely 10 square kilometres (around 6 miles) in area. The government of Qatar regarded the construction work as having gone against the GCC agreement to freeze the situation. It reacted by sending four armed helicopters to the construction site; some shots were fired, and the twenty-nine members of the team working there – two Englishmen, one Dutchman, two Thais and twenty-four Filipinos – were forcibly removed to Qatar. Qatar then declared the islet a Qatari 'exclusion zone', and both countries were reported to have started military preparations.

This was the most serious internal crisis in the young life of the GCC. It threatened to degenerate into an armed conflict between the two states, thereby forcing the member states to take sides. Moreover, hostilities of any kind in a region already suffering from the Iraq–Iran war would undermine the security of all the member states.

King Fahd of Saudi Arabia reacted swiftly to avert any further trouble. The following day he dispatched his Minister of Defence, Prince Sultan ibn Abdel Aziz, to mediate between the rulers of Qatar and Bahrain. As a result of Saudi negotiations with Shaikh Khalifah of Qatar and Shaikh Isa of Bahrain, the immediate crisis was resolved within a few days. An agreement between the two states worked out by Prince Sultan led to the withdrawal of Qatari troops from Fasht al-Dibal within a week; and, in mid-May, the kidnapped workers were returned to Bahrain.

Tension between the two countries remained high for some time, however. Bahrain accused Qatari aircraft and naval vessels of violating its air space and waters, and for a time Qatar banned all civilian airline flights over its territory. But before long, both countries accepted the Saudi proposals for an agreement to end the dispute. They agreed to restore the situation on Fasht al-Dibal to what it was before 26 April, and undertook not to use military force as long as efforts were under way to reach a solution.

Although a GCC commission was appointed to oversee the implementation of the agreement, there can be no doubt that the crisis was contained through Saudi efforts. Despite the many calls for restraint by the member states when the dispute first started, it ·was Saudi diplomacy which finally found the compromise solution. The Commission for the Settlement of Disputes between member states has yet to be institutionalized to the point of being effective. In the meantime, Saudi Arabia will continue to exert the greatest influence within the Gulf Cooperation Council.

The Iraq–Iran war

The war between the regional powers of Iraq and Iran is the first major conflagration to take place in the region since the days of the British Raj. The immediate cause was the lingering dispute – whose evolution can be traced back for a thousand years – over the delimitation of and right of access to the Shatt al-Arab estuary which forms the natural boundary between the two countries; the Iraqi claims to the Iranian province of Khuzestan (Arabistan to the Arabs), which is located on the river plain, were an extension of the same dispute. Although at first the hostilities were confined to specific areas within Iraq and Iran, they began to spread as the intensity of the fighting increased and as more and more countries became directly or indirectly involved. They inevitably reached the waters of the Gulf, and became a major threat to the economic lifeline of the Gulf states as well as to their very security. The political order established by the *pax Britannica* was in danger of being de-stabilized.

During the British period, the geo-political framework of the region had been based on the containment of Iraq, Iran and Saudi Arabia, which were all competing for influence. When, for example, Iraq tried to extend its influence to Kuwait during the late 1930s, discreet efforts were made by British political officers to turn Iraqi attention away from Kuwait and towards Khuzestan, which Iraq called Arabistan and regarded as Arab because of the presence of a large community there. Likewise, during the 1940s, 'an occasional mention of Arabistan Irredenta' to the Iranian government was thought of as sufficient to keep it in hand.[3]

To neutralize Iraq and Iran by directing their attention away from the Gulf states and towards the disputed province of Khuzestan was not formal British policy. Yet a Foreign Office official admitted in 1946 that: 'On "Arabistan" we cannot entirely exclude the possibility that we might be driven someday to consider stimulating a secessionist movement in SW Persia.'[4] It was however, regarded as a useful expedient if one of the two countries ever came to disturb the *status quo*. The separate and independent existence of the Gulf states was maintained, and the forward movements of the regional powers were absorbed into Britain's imperial requirements. As the Gulf states became the recipients of vast incomes from their petroleum reserves, they became even more vulnerable – particularly in view of their tiny populations – to the potential forces of the regional powers. At around the same time, Britain had started the process of giving independence to its former imperial possessions, which culminated in its withdrawal from the region.

Before leaving, however, Britain sought to ensure that as much as possible of the framework it had set up would remain stable in the wake of its withdrawal. To this end, it reached an agreement with the Shah regarding the sovereignty of Bahrain. It also provided Sultan Qaboos with the military aid and intelligence to combat the Dhufar Revolution. And it actively promoted the establishment of the UAE so that the member states would have a more secure structure within which to face the future.

Waiting in the wings, the USA viewed Britain's departure as the opportune moment to step forward and assert its presence. It had first started to work towards a forward policy in the Gulf during World War II; it then regarded the region's strategic position between Europe and the Pacific together with the importance of Saudi Arabia's oil resources as vital to the conduct of the war. But Britain stood firm in refusing it entry: in 1944, for example, it turned down the US request to establish a consulate in Bahrain, despite the close Anglo-American alliance. In 1950, a compromise on US representation was finally reached: the British government sanctioned the establishment of a US consulate in Kuwait, but continued to refuse a request for similar offices in the other Gulf states. It was not until independence in 1971 that US diplomatic ties with them were established.

Throughout the 1950s and 1960s, the Gulf region became increasingly important to the USA; but Britain's position there prevented it from exerting a corresponding influence. Because Britain and the USA were tested allies, the great rivalry between them in the Gulf remained muted. They worked together, for example, to return the Shah to power in the famous CIA coup of 1953. And they were both careful throughout the Buraimi crisis to act through second parties, thus maintaining their cordial ties.

In a way, the Suez war of 1956 can be regarded as a watershed in the relationship: in refusing to support Britain in its attack against Egypt, the USA undermined its ally's imperial position in the Arab world, thus hastening Britain's decline there; this paved the way for Britain's gradual replacement in Middle Eastern affairs – particularly in the Gulf – by the USA. The Eisenhower Doctrine was one of the first manifestations of this change.

The 'twin pillar' policy of the USA was implemented after 1971 when Britain left the region for good. It was maintained throughout the 1970s: the Shah acted as the 'policeman' of the Gulf, and in return obtained overwhelming US support. Iraq, which was receiving Soviet aid at this time, quietly sought to foster some form of regional integration with the Gulf states where it was determined to counteract Iranian influence. Both countries began actively to compete for hegemony once Britain evacuated the region.

When the Shah's regime collapsed in January 1979, so too did a vital component of US foreign policy. The consequent establishment of the Islamic Republic in Iran under the leadership of the Ayatollah Khomeini represented a major shift in the power structure of the region. Other events that same year caused the USA to search seriously for an alternative policy: the taking of hostages from the American embassy in Tehran, which signalled the staunch anti-American attitude of the new regime; the seizure of the Grand Mosque in Mecca, which was a major challenge to an important US ally; and the invasion of Afghanistan by Soviet forces, which were now closer than ever to the Gulf.

The importance of the region to the USA was underlined by President Carter in his January 1980 State of the Union address: 'Any attempt to gain control of the Persian Gulf region will be regarded as an assault on the vital interests of the United States of America.' The US Rapid Deployment Force (RDF), which had been established in December 1979, reflected a significant change in US policy. Whereas previously it had relied on the Shah militarily, the US now depended entirely on its own forces. This reliance was increased during the early days of the Reagan administration when a new permanent military command was created to protect US interests in the Gulf: this was the RDF Joint Task Force, which was much larger and more independent than the RDF. In 1983, it was transformed into the US Central Command

(USCENTCOM) administration. There could now be no doubt about American concern.

The USA was not alone in its views. The secular Baathist government of Iraq under President Saddam Hussein regarded the establishment of an Islamic republic on its borders with equal alarm. One of the dimensions of Iran's new forward policy was that it appealed to the religious sentiments of Shias throughout the Arab world (and beyond). And it called specifically on Iraq's substantial Shia population to bring about an Islamic revolution there.

The outbreak of war

Iraq was still chafing at the 1975 Algiers agreement which had been forced on it by the Shah; it saw in what it regarded as the post-revolutionary chaos of Iran a chance to be rid of its binding clauses. A collision course between the two countries was inevitable: it met on the cleavage plain of Khuzestan.

On 17 September 1980, Iraq abrogated the Algiers accord and five days later its forces invaded Iran. The war, which was to continue way beyond Iraq's original expectations, can be seen as the clash between many forces. It can be regarded as a modern manifestation of the ancient rivalry between the Arabs and the Persians; indeed, the Iraqi government has referred to it as Saddam Hussein's 'Qadissiyah', after the Arab victory over Persia in AD 637. It can also be regarded as a clash between a Shia revolutionary regime and a secular Baathist one. And it can be viewed as a struggle between two regional powers for hegemony over the Gulf. This was verified when, a few months before hostilities had started, Iraq warned Iran that it was prepared to send troops to protect Kuwait and Bahrain from any Iranian attempts at subversion.

The quick advances into Khuzestan by Iraqi forces during the first days of the war soon began to slow down as Iranian resistance gradually stiffened. By October, the war had taken on many of the characteristics of the trench battles of World War I. After Iraqi forces took the important Iranian cities of Abadan and Khorramshahr in November, a military stalemate between the two adversaries followed.

At this early stage of the war, two factors emerged: one was the superiority of the Iranian air force; and the other was the realization that the oil installations of both adversaries were important targets of attack. Iraq was the first to suffer significant losses: in November 1980, Iran put Iraq's oil-loading facilities in the Gulf out of action by bombing Fao and Mina al-Bakr. This cut Iraq's oil-exporting potential drastically and left it dependent on pipelines through Turkey and Syria; the latter country, however, as a major ally of Iran, refused to allow the passage of Iraqi oil. The pipeline through Turkey became the only conduit.

On the first anniversary of the war, in September 1981, Iranian forces took back Abadan in a major reversal. Heavy fighting followed, with huge loss of life on both sides. This major Iranian victory paved the way for the recapture of Khorramshahr seven months later and the ultimate withdrawal of Iraqi forces from Iranian territory.

By the summer of 1982, as the war of attrition continued in a depressing human tragedy, thousands were dead, hundreds of thousands were wounded and there were as many prisoners of war. Several new factors emerged. Iran now had the military initiative, but its air power was declining seriously as the US government refused to sanction the replacement of equipment in what had been an essentially American-made air force. Iran's use at this time of human-wave tactics demonstrated the ability of the regime to sustain casualties. Iraq, on the other hand, had a superior supply of weaponry, and continued to receive supplies from the USSR. Militarily it was on the defensive, and its oil-exporting facilities – in contrast to those of Iran – had declined drastically.

In August 1982, Iran mounted a strong attack on Basra, Iraq's second biggest city, which has a large Shia population. Iraqi resistance at this time revealed to the Iranians that there was no 'fifth column' of Shias in the Iraqi army; just as the Arabs in Khuzestan had earlier proved loyal to Iran, so too did the Shias of Iraq demonstrate that their nationalism was stronger than religious affiliation.

The fighting continued. In late September 1982, Iran launched an unsuccessful attack on Baghdad. As the Iranian offensives continued and as Iraqi defensive positions hardened, a new factor emerged: Iraq now had undoubted air supremacy. This was reinforced when France said it would lend Iraq five super *étendard* naval fighters with the Exocet missiles Argentina had used so effectively during the 1982 Falkland islands war with Britain. The conflict over oil installations now expanded, with the Iraqi air force regularly attacking Kharj island oil terminal, one of the most important in the world. When in April 1983 the Iranian forces launched another offensive, Iraq responded by attacking tankers and oil facilities in the Gulf. The 'tanker war' had begun, and with it, the spread of fighting to the waters of the Gulf.

Early GCC reactions

The Gulf states viewed the various phases of the war with increasing apprehension. Although at first they tended to regard the fighting as almost peripheral, it was not long before its repercussions dominated regional politics. During the first days of the war, the Iraqi government had demanded the return of the Tunb and Abu Musa islands which the Shah had seized from the UAE on the eve of the British withdrawal. This demand appears to have been dropped, but the Gulf states were not totally ignored during the early phases of the fighting. Two Kuwaiti border posts were attacked by Iranian aircraft in November 1980, a few weeks after hostilities had started; this was a clear warning to the Gulf states not to support Iraq in too obvious a manner.

One of the first and most important reactions of the Gulf states to the war was the establishment of the GCC. And those states – Saudi Arabia, Kuwait, Qatar and the UAE – which could afford it, agreed to help Iraq financially, particularly after its oil-exporting facilities were crippled; by 1983, they had lent Iraq around $24 billion. As the war progressed, the sums given grew accordingly, with Kuwait and Saudi Arabia donating the largest amounts. Because the price of oil fell drastically at around the same time, the Gulf states began to feel the pinch of recession acutely; in Kuwait, Bahrain and the UAE, this was compounded by the Suq al-Manakh crisis. Budget deficits were declared; many big projects were reduced in size; austerity measures of all kinds were introduced which forced cutbacks in spending. As a result, financial aid to the rest of the Arab world had to be reduced radically. Kuwait, for example, cut 39 per cent of its aid to Jordan, Syria and the PLO because of its budget deficit; the war in the Gulf took precedence over the war with Israel, and by 1987 it had ceased to provide Syria – Iran's ally – with aid.

The Gulf states continued to hover rather nervously on the edges of the war. In December 1981, they were shaken by the discovery of a coup attempt in Bahrain which had clear links with Tehran. There followed the bi-lateral security agreements which they all – with the exception of Kuwait – signed with Saudi Arabia. Saudi Arabia also attempted to persuade Syria – unsuccessfully as it turned out – to open its pipeline to Iraqi oil. At this time Kuwait was actively engaged with Algeria in seeking a diplomatic solution to the war. While Iraq had already expressed its willingness to negotiate, Iran's preconditions for any kind of peace talks made them impossible: these included international condemnation of Iraq as the initial aggressor, the fall of Saddam Hussein's government and the payment of war reparations from Iraq of up to $150 billion.

Although the Gulf states were providing Iraq – as a fellow Arab state – with financial aid, they were careful otherwise to take as neutral a stand as possible during the early years of the war. On the one hand, they were clearly ill equipped and unwilling to become militarily involved. On the other, there was still some trepidation, particularly in Kuwait, regarding Iraqi ambitions in the region as a whole. In July 1981, for example, Iraq officially re-stated its request to lease Bubiyan island; the issue had been dormant since 1977, and now raised the possibility of new tensions between Kuwait and Baghdad.

Thus when the GCC had its summit meeting in November 1982, it carefully chose the wording of its official communiqué. It gave great weight to the importance of peace initiatives; the Council assured Iraq of its total support in its efforts to find a peaceful solution to the conflict. In November 1983, after it had acquired naval fighters from France, Iraq started to raid Iranian ships sailing in Iranian waters; several Iranian warships were sunk. Two Greek tankers carrying Iranian oil were also attacked. In retaliation, Iran began to focus its threats on the Gulf states.

Threats to internal security

A period of threats to internal security followed in Qatar and Kuwait. In early November 1983, arms and ammunition were discovered in Doha; they were said to have been placed there in an attempt to assassinate the heads of state in the forthcoming GCC summit meeting in Qatar.

In December 1983, Kuwait was rocked by a series of bomb attacks. The main targets were the US and French embassies, a residential area in which US nationals live, the control tower of the airport and a power station, but the real focus of the bombers was undoubtedly US and French interests. The techniques used were similar to those which had destroyed the US and French forces headquarters in Beirut earlier that year, although the amount of explosives was far less. The mysterious Islamic Jihad movement, which is believed to have connections with the Shia opposition in Iraq (the Da'wa Party) as well as with Shia groups in Lebanon, claimed responsibility for the attacks.

Many different aspects of regional politics were brought into focus with the bombings. They underlined the vulnerable position of Kuwait in the Iraq–Iran war and acted to drive a wedge between the Shia and Sunni populations there. They were a sharp reminder of the links with the civil war in Lebanon, and of the importance of the Iranian revolution in the daily lives of the people of the Gulf states. On the international level, they re-affirmed Iranian hostility towards US and French policies in the region.

The sequel to the attacks provided a link with Kuwaiti affairs which went well beyond the shores of the Gulf. Seventeen young men – of whom two were Lebanese Shias – were arrested and sentenced to death for the bombings; the sentences were not carried out, but the men remained in prison. The kidnapping of westerners – including the Archbishop of Canterbury's emissary, Terry Waite – in Beirut was directly connected to the continued detention of the seventeen men; their release from jail has been a precondition for the release of the hostages in Beirut. In late 1984, a Kuwait Airways aircraft was hijacked to Tehran in another attempt to have the seventeen men released. Although Colonel Oliver North admitted in his testimony before the Select Committee of the House and Senate (the Irangate hearings) that he had advocated their release in order to extricate the western hostages from Lebanon, Kuwait has remained firm in its refusal to do so.

Kuwait is undoubtedly the most vulnerable Gulf state. Its proximity to the battle zone is such that the sound of fighting can be heard in Kuwait city. Moreover, it provides Iraq, whose ports in the Gulf have been paralysed by the fighting, with trans-shipment facilities. It has no export pipelines at a safe distance from the battle zone; it therefore relies exclusively on ships sailing the entire length of the Gulf to its loading points. It has always taken a neutral stand in cold war politics and has generally relied on diplomatic – rather than military – means for its defence. It had hitherto considered its neutral and independent position as its greatest strength, but the war between Iraq and Iran ultimately caused it to reconsider its options.

When, in May 1984, two Kuwaiti tankers were hit by missiles in the Gulf, Kuwait blamed Iran. The next month, it arrested four Iranians for sabotage; bomb materials had been found in their possession. Kuwaiti tankers were not the only ones being attacked in Gulf waters at this time. A number of Saudi ships were hit as well. President Reagan announced shortly after this that there was only a 'very slight' chance of US military aid to protect Gulf shipping. In early June, therefore, Saudi warplanes, guided by US AWAC radar aircraft, shot down an Iranian airplane flying in Saudi air space. The Kuwaiti government requested Stinger missiles from the USA in an effort to install some form of military capability which could be as effective as that of Saudi Arabia. The US Congress refused to sanction the missiles, but agreed instead to sell anti-aircraft equipment.

The vulnerable position of Kuwait was again emphasized in May 1985 when a car bomb exploded near the motorcade of the Amir, Shaikh Jabir al-Ahmad. Almost miraculously the Amir escaped with only minor injuries. A few months later, bombs went off in two seaside cafés, this time claiming many lives.

At the November 1985 summit of the GCC, a new attitude of the rulers towards the war was registered. It was expressed in very subtle language, but its meaning was unmistakable. The Gulf states and Saudi Arabia wanted to take a more neutral stand towards Iran. This had been preceded by quiet diplomatic initiatives by Iranian officials who sought to improve their relationship with the member states of the GCC, with the possible exception of Kuwait. The visit of the Saudi Foreign Minister, Prince Saud al-Faisal, to Tehran earlier in 1985 bore witness to the change; it was followed by a return visit from his Iranian counterpart. It has been suggested that the Saudi government in 1986 dismissed the oil minister, Shaikh Ahmed Yamani, in response to a request by the Iranians who objected to his policies. An uneasy relationship between Iran and Saudi Arabia was maintained, and the GCC remained nervously neutral as a result.

Irangate

On the ground, major developments in the fighting occurred in February 1986 when Iranian forces captured Fao; the next day they reached the Kuwaiti border on the Gulf. Iraq denied that Fao had fallen and claimed instead that it had crushed the Iranian advance. Four days later, on 15 February, the *Washington Post*, quoting 'sources with satellite photographs' denied the claims of both parties; it said that there had been little change on the ground.

This marked another significant departure in the course of the war. The undeniable Iranian victory in Fao brought the Iranian army closer to the Gulf states than ever before; Iranian missiles in Fao could reach Kuwait with ease. Fears of an ultimate Iraqi defeat also abounded at this time, for it had lost an integral part of its territory. Equally important was the strange message emanating from the *Washington Post*: why did those 'satellite sources' misread such an obviously major battle?

It was not until the *Al-Shira'a* (a Lebanese weekly) revealed in early November 1986 that senior US officials had gone on a secret mission to Tehran – to make available spare parts and ammunition in exchange for the release of American hostages in Lebanon – that this question began to be answered. For in uncovering what came to be known as 'Irangate', *Al Shira'a* started the process of unravelling some of the mysteries of the conflicting attitudes taken by the USA – and others – towards the war.

The two most significant of these reveal a certain cynicism which is reminiscent of some aspects of the British approach towards neutralizing the powers of Iraq and Iran during the 1930s and 1940s. The first of these was succinctly put in a statement made by a senior US statesman. When asked his view of the Iraq–Iran war, he answered 'A pity only one side can lose.' As information on US attitudes about the war began to filter out after the revelations of Irangate, this perception was verified.

On 12 January 1987, an article in *The New York Times*, quoting 'intelligence sources', claimed that the USA had provided both sides with deliberately distorted data. Although this was denied by the CIA, earlier revelations had confirmed the general policy. While the USA had been secretly supplying Iran with arms, the CIA had been providing the Iraqi air force with sensitive satellite pictures of Iranian targets. An American government source at the time claimed that the US administration was engaged in 'a cynical attempt to engineer a stalemate' between the two antagonists.[5] It is interesting to note here that President Saddam Hussein had already accused the USA, as far back as November 1982, of having a policy which was for a continuation of the war; he was then speaking at a press conference for US newsmen in Baghdad. It is also interesting to note an article in *The New York Times*[6] just a few weeks after the war had started. It asserted that the Iraqi battle plan for the initial invasion had originally been drawn up with British help around 1950, when Iraq had been in close alliance with Britain, and that its ultimate objective had been the conquest of Khuzestan.

During his testimony before the Select Committee of the House and Senate in July 1987, Colonel Oliver North admitted that during his secret talks with Iranian officials, he had indicated that the USA would be willing to overthrow Saddam Hussein.[7] The USA was not alone in dealing thus with both sides. In December 1986, for example, a Foreign Office official in London admitted that both Iraqi and Iranian officers were receiving training in Britain.[8] He went on to qualify this by adding that the training was essentially non-combatant.

The second attitude, however, is even more cynical; for it goes beyond the objectives of geo-politics. It can be deduced from the bits of information which – for one reason or another – have been made available on arms sales to the combatants during the course of the war. It reveals the extraordinary profits which arms merchants – and indirectly, their countries – have enjoyed. Although no data on these arms sales can be complete, enough estimates have been made to provide a strong indication of the financial rewards involved. *The Financial Times*[9] estimated that between 1979 and 1983, Iraq bought arms worth $17.6 billion; and during the same period, Iranian purchases amounted to $5.4 billion. Iraq's main suppliers for those years were: the USSR ($7.2 billion); France ($3.8 billion); China ($1.5 billion) and Poland ($0.9 billion). Iran's for the same period were: the USA ($2.4 billion); France ($1.2 billion); Britain ($0.6 billion); and China ($0.3 billion).

A cursory glance at that list of eight countries immediately reveals that France and China were supplying both sides with weaponry. Other sources maintain that no less than twenty-seven countries have been supplying both Iraq and Iran with the arms and ammunition to keep the war alive. They are led by the USA and the USSR. The latter has been supplying Iran directly and through its allies, such as North Korea, Poland, Czechoslovakia and Romania. The USA, contravening its own embargo, sold weaponry to Iran in 1985–6 directly and indirectly through Israel.[10] An interesting example is the case of Italy. Although the government there declared that it was in favour of an arms embargo to both sides in 1984, thirty-nine authorizations were given to export arms to both sides.[11]

The war has also stimulated the Gulf states and Saudi Arabia to purchase huge amounts of arms in an effort to defend themselves in case of a spill-over of fighting. Since they all have enormous budgets for defence, arms manufacturers and dealers have once again reaped great financial rewards. Exact figures on these sales are, of course, not available, but they are known to run into billions of US dollars.

Until 1987, the war had provoked little more than international indifference. That year, however, the revelations of the Irangate hearings and the gradual dissemination of information about arms supplies focused world attention on the conflict. The untold human suffering, the mounting losses on both sides, the number of maimed and wounded, and the continued devastation of towns and villages finally found sympathy world-wide.

Hitherto, the indifference had followed the realization that the war would not affect the regular flow of oil from either country. When the oil-loading facilities at Kharj island became impossible to use, Iran re-located at Sirri island, near the mouth of the Gulf and outside the Iraqi air force's range; its tankers continued to export around 3 million barrels a day. Likewise, Iraq opened a new pipeline through Saudi Arabia in late 1985, and another through Turkey to ensure the flow of oil. When the tanker war started, there were new fears about oil supplies, for over 300 tankers were hit and a number of sailors killed. But that did not stop the continued entry of tankers to the Gulf, despite the high risks.

Once the implications of Irangate began to be realized, together with a growing awareness of the great financial rewards of the arms suppliers, the international attitude towards the war underwent a perceptible change. One of the manifestations of this change was the unanimous vote in the United Nations Security Council in July 1987 for Resolution 598, which called for a ceasefire. The

Secretary General followed this up by a visit to Iraq and Iran two months later.

Diverging attitudes

In the meantime, Kuwait was subject to an increasing number of acts of sabotage. In January 1987, three fires broke out at one of Kuwait's oil complexes. Three days later, a shell landed on Failaka island, a short distance from Kuwait city. That same week, a car bomb exploded in downtown Kuwait; although no casualties were reported, there was considerable damage. Security forces reported shortly afterwards that the fires in the oil complex had been started deliberately. Sixteen men were accused of both the arson and bomb attacks; of these, some were Kuwaiti Shias of Iranian origin.

One of the most serious consequences of the war in the Gulf states has been the creation of the concept that their Shia citizens could potentially become Iran's 'fifth column'. This concept has gone a long way to weakening social cohesion, particularly in Kuwait and Bahrain. It will take some time to overcome once the war is over, for it has brought with it mutual suspicions which cannot be quickly forgotten.

Although Dubai, in the UAE, has a large Shia population which is Iranian in origin – rather than Arab as in Kuwait and Bahrain – the concept of the 'fifth column' is very weak. Dubai – and, to a lesser extent, Sharjah, its closest neighbour – have enjoyed a brisk and lively trade with Iran during most of the war. They have revived their previous roles as major entrepôts of trade and created a new one as suppliers of services. Their dhows have been plying back and forth to the Iranian coast laden with a wide variety of consumer goods, foodstuffs and equipment of all kinds. Although most of their cargoes are banned in Iran in order to preserve foreign currency, the seamen of Dubai and Sharjah manage to get them through undetected. The profits are considerable, both to individual traders and to the economies of Dubai and Sharjah. Another lucrative activity has been in servicing international shipping which finds Dubai a safer place than Kuwait or Iranian ports. There has been an added bonus: Dubai's dry dock – one of the largest in the world and until recently considered to be a white elephant – is busy maintaining and overhauling tankers as well as repairing those damaged in the fighting.

Dubai and Sharjah are therefore loath to relinquish their

neutrality in the war. Moreover, Sharjah has an agreement with Iran regarding the oil resources of Abu Musa island which has been maintained despite the fall of the Shah; good relations with Iran are therefore important for the continuation of the agreement. Both Sharjah and Dubai are far enough away from the battlefield not to feel threatened by the possibility of a spill-over. Abu Dhabi does not necessarily share the same attitude. Shaikh Zayid, its ruler, who is also President of the UAE, has been outspoken in his support of a pan-Arab stand towards the war, thus favouring Iraq. In November 1986, two missiles hit an offshore oilfield in Abu Dhabi; both Iraq and Iran denied having fired them. A week later, Iran, obviously anxious to maintain good relations with the UAE, offered to help in the repair of the field. The fact that the population of the UAE is made up of both Arabs (the large majority) and Iranians (a significant minority) underlines its desire to maintain good relations with both sides. Significantly, a Sharjah newspaper, the *Al-Khaleej*, was the only one to publish the entire text of the Gulf war report purportedly made by the Secretary General of the United Nations after a visit there in September 1987.[12] The report had been kept secret, but its publication revealed Iran's willingness to negotiate through the United Nations for a just and lasting peace settlement. This contradicted earlier reports on the difficulties of the Secretary General's mission caused by Iranian intransigence.

Qatar and Oman also favour maintaining good relations with Iran. Like the UAE, Qatar has an important Iranian community. Oman is a close neighbour of Iran: its easternmost tip on the Straits of Hormuz is not far away from the coast of Iran across the water. It has a long history of good relations with Iran – most recently, the Shah's aid was vital to Sultan Qaboos's victory in Dhufar. Oman's firm belief in the importance of maintaining a position of neutrality in the GCC has coloured many of the meetings of the Council.

Throughout 1987, Kuwait, Bahrain and Saudi Arabia found themselves on one side and the other four members of the GCC on the other regarding their respective stand towards Iran. As Iranian attacks on tankers using Kuwaiti ports increased – by September, the number had reached fifty-six, seven of which were Kuwaiti-owned – Kuwait felt increasingly isolated. The acts of sabotage also continued. In April, a car bomb exploded outside the Kuwait Petroleum Company. In May, another bomb was set off in Kuwait city; and a fire – suspected to have been caused by arsonists – broke out in an oil complex.

Re-flagging operations

In a unilateral move which startled many observers, Kuwait decided to take action to protect at least its fleet of tankers. Unable to provide the necessary military strength itself, it approached the five permanent members of the Security Council – the USA, the USSR, China, Britain and France – for help, requesting that Kuwaiti tankers re-register and sail under their flags. This was preceded by a period of uncertainty: the USA claimed that Kuwait had originally approached it in late 1986; Kuwait denied this claim. Other reports stated that Kuwait had indeed requested the USA to re-flag its vessels and that at first it had hesitated; the USSR was said to have immediately agreed to place three Soviet tankers at Kuwait's disposal. This stimulated the USA to dispatch its own naval vessels to the Gulf and to re-flag 11 Kuwaiti tankers. In any case, further developments in the war quickly put an end to this form of speculation.

On 17 May 1987, an Iraqi Exocet missile accidentally hit the USS *Stark*, which was sailing around 130 kilometres (80 miles) off Bahrain; thirty-seven American servicemen were killed. The US government responded in a surprising fashion: rather than blame the country which had fired the missile, it castigated Iran for the disruption to international shipping. In the meantime, the Joint Chiefs of Staff recommended to President Reagan that, in order to protect re-flagged Kuwaiti tankers, the US naval presence in the Gulf would have to be expanded.

This recommendation was made at a time when reports of a new arms delivery to Iran from China – including a battery of Silkworm missiles – were being made, together with news of a Soviet *rapprochement*. One of the interesting features of the war has been the changes made by the two superpowers in their respective alliances. When the war started, Iraq was firmly in the Soviet orbit, relying heavily on the USSR for its military equipment. It had severed diplomatic ties with the USA after the June 1967 Arab–Israeli war because of the close American–Israeli alliance. But by 1984, these alliances had shifted. Iraq and the USA renewed their diplomatic relations, and within three years, Iraq had become America's third largest trading partner in the

Middle East, after Saudi Arabia and Egypt. In August 1987, Iraq and the USA signed an agreement to strengthen their economic relations. As a result, Iraq bought basic foodstuffs at low prices from the USA which also provided the credit facilities. Iran had earlier been antagonistic to the USSR. But a *rapprochement* between the two surfaced in 1987, for in October they signed a treaty of friendship and cooperation which covered collaboration in a number of fields.

The summer of 1987 was a particularly hot one in the region: the temperatures soared well above normal and the humidity was uncomfortably high. The focus, however, was not so much on the temperature, but on the heat generated by the growing armada of foreign ships in the Gulf against a background of reiterated Iranian threats against interference. The American fleet in and around the Gulf gradually grew to such an extent that it was said to be the largest such assembly abroad since the Vietnam war. It included thirty ships – battleships, carriers, frigates, minesweepers and support vessels – and at least 30,000 men. The American fleet was not alone: it was joined by frigates, minesweepers, destroyers and support vessels of Belgium, Holland, France, Italy and Britain; and a Soviet fleet of frigates and minesweepers was also present. The US navy began to escort re-flagged Kuwaiti tankers in July.

The Mecca riots

That same month, an event occurred on the western coast of Saudi Arabia, far from the assembling ships of the world's most powerful navies, which was to have an equally significant impact on the Islamic world. On 31 July 1987, Mecca was the scene of angry demonstrations which resulted in the deaths of several hundred people. This took place during the annual Hajj (pilgrimage) when the city was crowded with pilgrims from all over the world. Although details of the actual events have conflicted radically according to the source of reports, it is clear that Iranian pilgrims assembled near the Grand Mosque and led a demonstration which protested against the USA, the USSR and Israel. The Saudi authorities had previously banned any kind of political demonstration during the Hajj, so they called their security forces in. According to one version (Iranian), the police opened fire on Iranian pilgrims, and some 600 people were killed and another

2,000 were wounded. Another version (Saudi) was that Saudi forces attempted to restrain the Iranian demonstration; they used tear gas, but were otherwise unarmed. The ensuing panic amongst the huge crowds – 2 million pilgrims were in Mecca that year – caused many to be trampled in the crush. The Saudi authorities acknowledged that 402 people were killed, of which a large proportion were Iranians.

This one event probably did more to mobilize widespread popular feeling against the Islamic Republic of Iran than had all the years of war with Iraq. Horror and outrage at the disturbances at Islam's holiest shrine were expressed throughout the Arab world, and much of it was directed at the Iranians. Saudi Arabia could no longer remain hesitant in its policies towards Iran; the uneasy relationship of the past two years was abruptly terminated. Attitudes inevitably hardened two days later when the Saudi and Kuwaiti embassies in Tehran were attacked and occupied.

Diplomatic initiative

The Mecca crisis was a catalyst in the process of unifying divergent Arab positions. It was no longer possible to remain a neutral bystander. During the Foreign Ministers' meeting of the GCC in October 1987, the final statement reflected Saudi anger and a new determination to express it, despite earlier considerations. Iranian aggression against Kuwait – a Silkworm missile had been fired at a floating oil-loading terminal a few days earlier – was seen as a dangerous escalation; the unity of the GCC was confirmed in a reminder that aggression against one member state was equivalent to aggression against them all.

At almost the same time, rumours began to circulate that Egypt was about to send military assistance, including seventy pilots, to Kuwait. Egypt's membership of the Arab League had been suspended in 1979 following the Camp David Peace Agreement, yet it had supported Iraq throughout the war. But its open alliance with Kuwait, if true, revealed a radical change of Arab policy towards Egypt.

The meeting of Arab heads of state, convened by the Arab League in Amman in early November 1987 had been preceded by Jordanian diplomatic efforts. These involved convincing President Hafez al-Assad of Syria, the main Arab ally of Iran, to attend; and, having done so, to establish some form of reconciliation between his country and Iraq. The continuing feud between those two countries had been a significant impediment in previous Arab summits to the formation of a united stand against Iran.

At the Amman summit, however, the twenty-two Arab leaders appeared to have closed ranks. The final communiqué unanimously condemned Iran for its continued intransigence regarding a ceasefire and for its continued occupation of Iraqi territory. It expressed strong support for Saudi Arabia and Kuwait in the face of Iranian threats. And it sanctioned the resumption of relations with Egypt, thus allowing Kuwait to accept Egyptian military assistance.

The Amman summit represented a milestone in Arab politics. For the first time, the Gulf states occupied the centre stage. Until then, their role had been confined to one of providing financial aid to the less wealthy members of the Arab League and to maintaining the unity of the organization in the face of disruptive forces. Hitherto, they had been called on for help. This time, the summit was convened on their behalf: this time they called on the Arab League to reciprocate, and in so doing, the twenty-two heads of state acknowledged that the security of its eastern flank was vital to the stability of the Arab world.

Options and strategic choices

The most important objective of the Gulf states throughout the war has been to maintain their internal stability and external security. This includes, of course, their ability to ship their oil and utilize the international waters of the Gulf without risk. The prime strategic means to secure this goal was to establish a framework within which to confront the inherent dangers of the conflict.

The creation of the GCC a few months after the outbreak of the war was the concrete expression of this strategic means. It was an implicit recognition of both the paramount importance of Saudi Arabia and the inherent limitations of the military capabilities of the member states. Since its establishment, the GCC has been characterized by its ability to maintain a united front despite the difference in attitudes towards Iraq and Iran. This unity has allowed the organization to survive and to explore effectively the various available options.

The first of these options was to provide Iraq with financial and economic aid. Iraq is a fellow Arab state, a fellow member of the

Arab League and a fellow signatory of the defence agreement of the League. It also belongs to many of the social, cultural and economic organizations which were founded in the Gulf during the 1970s. At the beginning of the war, four member states of the GCC provided it with aid: Saudi Arabia, Kuwait, the UAE and Qatar. As the war progressed, the first two became the principal donors. And as a result, Iran has focused its attacks on Kuwait because of its continued support of Iraq.

The framework of the GCC has provided the member states with another option: to maintain contact with Iran at the same time. Oman and the UAE have enjoyed good relations with Iran throughout the war; the argument has been that to continue a dialogue with Iran will make a negotiated peace settlement more likely. It is significant that Iran was neither criticized nor condemned at a GCC summit held in Riyadh a month after the Amman Arab League summit. Moreover, the *Observer* reported on 20 September 1987 a 'secret' Arab peace plan. This entailed the payment to Iran of \$50 billion as war reparations; and the promise that the GCC would remain neutral both *vis-à-vis* Iraq and Iran and towards the superpowers once hostilities ended. It is still too early to ascertain the validity of such a report, but it is clear that in maintaining open channels of communication with Iran, the GCC has exercised a valuable option.

Although it was Kuwait alone which approached the USA to re-flag its vessels, its fellow members in the GCC were careful not to denounce this option which it had chosen to exercise. This preserved the unity of the organization. The massive US presence in the Gulf, together with the ships of other western navies, has undoubtedly acted to contain the fighting and prevent it from spreading beyond Iraq and Iran.

Kuwait approached the USSR for help at the same time. Although it was the only GCC country to have diplomatic relations with the USSR when the war broke out in 1980, three more states have since joined it: Oman, the UAE and Qatar. It is still, of course, too early to predict whether Saudi Arabia is about to change its policy towards the USSR. The visit to Moscow of its Foreign Minister, Prince Saud al-Faisal, in January 1988, is, however, a significant departure, for in attempting to normalize relations with the superpowers, Saudi Arabia has strengthened the unity of the GCC.

The resumption of Arab relations with Egypt, which was

promoted by the GCC at the Amman summit, was another important option. It has provided the member states with the support of the leading Arab country, which is prepared to give them access to its large supply of military manpower. It has also ascertained the ability of the GCC to sway Arab regional politics. And it has fulfilled a long-standing objective of the USA – whose fleet is protecting Kuwaiti shipping – by lifting the isolation of Egypt in the Arab world.

Based on its present characteristics, there are a number of possible scenarios for the ending of the war. These include: a victory for one of the two countries; a continuing stalemate so that the war will finally peter out; and/or a negotiated peace settlement along the lines of United Nations Resolution 598. Much will depend on which of the two will have the longest staying power. But regardless of which scenario is proven correct, one factor is likely to remain constant: the Gulf states, through the GCC and the exercising of the available options, are in a position to safeguard their national interests and to have a say in determining the final outcome.

* * * *

There have been many phases in the protracted conflict between Iran and Iraq. During the first year of hostilities, Iraq seemed to have gained the upper hand after occupying large tracts of Iran. Iranian forces started to turn back the tide a year later. After taking back all captured territory, they went on to conquer parts of Iraq, culminating in the capture of Fao in 1986. Two years later, the tide had turned yet again and it was Iraq's turn to take the military initiative and recapture lost lands. In the meantime, outside involvement, which had started in a low key, almost surreptitious manner, culminated in the arrival of a massive foreign armada in and around the waters of the Gulf. And a new phase appears to have started as this book goes to press: the sudden Iranian acceptance in July 1988 of United Nations Resolution 598, which calls for a ceasefire, has made a negotiated peace settlement seem more likely.

As the fortunes of the combatants fluctuated, the Gulf states adjusted with caution and pragmatism. At first, they were content to remain apart. Inevitably, however, they were gradually drawn into the periphery of the conflict, the case of Kuwait being the most notable. All – to varying degrees – have witnessed local reactions to the war which have been exacerbated by the economic recession. The Gulf states are still extremely wealthy, but their diminished incomes have made them more prudent consumers. And the long war has induced them to spend considerable sums of money to upgrade their own armies and defence forces.

Although the war itself has inevitably introduced many changes, certain features appear to have remained stable. The structure of the Gulf states, for example, has not altered; their political systems and their boundaries have been maintained.

Moreover, these states have continued their socio-economic development despite the many dramatic events taking place around them. This is manifested in many ways, not least in the process which began with independence to institutionalize a variety of activities. For example, the Kuwait Fund for Arab Economic Development continues to provide aid to developing countries; the Kuwait Institute for Scientific Research to sponsor research in power systems and information technology; the Arab Gulf Thought Forum to stimulate young intellectuals; the offshore banks of Bahrain their international operations; the Dubai Chamber of Commerce to promote regional and international trade; and the universities in all the Gulf states to expand in number and size. The list is long.

Despite the apparent growth of local nationalism – of which the movements for 'Kuwaitization', 'Bahrainization', etc. are an indication – the established pattern of the 1970s of building strong bridges with the rest of the Arab world has been maintained.

The presence of foreign navies in Gulf waters is another indication of historical continuity, albeit of a different kind. Particularly revealing has been the fact that US naval forces were mobilized to sustain the 'maritime peace' of the 1980s, echoing the actions of the British Indian fleet in the nineteenth century.

The most striking feature of all perhaps is that the essential geo-political characteristics of the region have remained unchanged. Despite some almost apocalyptic episodes in the fighting – oil tankers ablaze in the Gulf, trench warfare on a scale unknown since World War I, US helicopters in pitched battle with Iranian naval forces – the order laid down by the *pax Britannica* has survived the momentous events of the 1980s.

Notes

1 Anthony H. Cordesman, *The Gulf and the Search for Strategic Stability* (Colorado, 1984), p. 626.
2 Interview in *The Middle East*, November 1983.
3 Public Record Office, London. F0371/52313. E4949/187/65. Minute by J. T. Henderson, 3 June 1946.
4 Public Record Office, London. F0371/52313. E3856/181/65. Minute by L. F. Pynne, 4 May 1946.
5 *The Independent*, 16 December 1986.
6 16 October 1980.
7 *The Independent*, 11 July 1987.
8 *The Independent*, 25 July 1987.
9 15 August 1987.
10 See Frank Barnaby, 'The Gulf's seven-year boom', *South*, May 1987.
11 Reported in *The Independent*, 18 August 1987.
12 Excerpts translated in *The Independent*, 19 September 1987.

Appendix: The Ministers of the Gulf States

The Council of Ministers of Kuwait

*Members of the Al Sabah family

Prime Minister and Crown Prince	SHAIKH SAAD AL-ABDALLAH*
Deputy Prime Minister and Minister of Foreign Affairs	SHAIKH SABAH AL-AHMAD*
Minister of Education	Anwar Abdallah Al-Nouri
Minister of Social Affairs and Labour	SHAIKH NASIR MUHAMMAD AL-AHMAD*
Minister of Finance	Jasim Muhammad al-Khurafi
Minister of Awqaf and Islamic Affairs	Khalid Ahmad al-Jassar
Minister of Communications	Abdallah A. Al-Sharhan
Minister of State for Cabinet Affairs	Rashid Abdel Aziz al-Rashid
Minister of Defence	SHAIKH NAWWAF AL-AHMAD AL-JABIR*
Minister of State for Foreign Affairs	Saud Muhammad al-Osaimi
Minister of Justice and Legal Affairs	Dhari Abdallah al-Othman
Minister of Public Works	Abdel Rahman Ibrahim al-Huti
Minister of State for Municipality Affairs	Muhammad Sayyid Abdel Muhsin Al-Rifai
Minister of Public Health	Dr Abdel Razzaq Y. Al-Abdel Razzaq
Minister of Oil	SHAIKH ALI AL-KHALIFAH AL-ATHBI*

Minister of State for Services Affairs	Isa Muhammad al-Mazeidi
Minister of Commerce and Industry	Faisal Abdel-Razzaq al-Khalid
Minister of Planning	Dr Abdel Rahman A. Al-Awadi
Minister of Electricity and Water	Dr Hamoud Abdallah Al-Ruqba
Minister of the Interior	SHAIKH SALIM SABAH AL-SALIM*
Minister of State for Housing Affairs	Nasir Abdallah al-Rudhan
Minister of Information	SHAIKH JABIR MUBARAK AL-HAMAD*

The Council of Ministers of Bahrain

*Members of the Al Khalifah family

Prime Minister	SHAIKH KHALIFAH BIN SALMAN*
Minister of Foreign Affairs	SHAIKH MUHAMMAD BIN MUBARAK*
Minister of the Interior	SHAIKH KHALIFAH BIN MUHAMMAD*
Minister of Justice and Islamic Affairs	SHAIKH ABDALLAH BIN KHALID*
Minister of Labour	SHAIKH KHALIFAH BIN SALMAN*
Minister of Housing	SHAIKH KHALID BIN ABDALLAH*
Minister of Education	Dr Ali Muhammad Fakhro
Minister of Development and Industry	Yusif Ahmad Shirawi
Minister of Finance and Economy	Ibrahim Muhammad Abdel Karim
Minister of Health	Jawad Salim Urayidh
Minister of Works, Electricity and Water	Majid Jawad al-Jishi
Minister of Communications	Ibrahim Humeidan

Minister of Commerce and Agriculture	H. Ahmad Qasim
Minister of State for Legal Affairs	Husain M. al-Baharna
Minister of State for Cabinet Affairs (Acting)	Yusif Ahmad Shirawi
Director of the Organization Youth and Sports	SHAIKH ALI BIN MUHAMMAD*
Minister of Information	Tariq Mu'ayyad
Director of Municipality Affairs	SHAIKH ABDALLAH BIN MUHAMMAD*
Director of the Civil Service	SHAIKH ALI BIN ALI BIN MUHAMMAD*

The Council of Ministers of Qatar

*Members of the Al Thani family

Prime Minister	HH The Amir*
Minister of Defence and C-in-C of the Armed Forces	SHAIKH HAMAD BIN KHALIFAH*
Minister of Education, Youth and Welfare	SHAIKH MUHAMMAD BIN HAMAD*
Minister of the Interior	SHAIKH KHALID BIN HAMAD*
Minister of Finance and Petroleum	SHAIKH ABDEL AZIZ BIN KHALIFAH*
Minister of Water and Electricity	SHAIKH JASIM BIN MUHAMMAD*
Minister of Industry and Agriculture	SHAIKH FAISAL BIN THANI*
Minister of State for Foreign Affairs	SHAIKH AHMAD BIN SAIF*
Speaker of Advisory Council	Abdel Aziz bin Khalid al-Ghanim
Adviser to HH The Amir	Dr Hasan Kamil
Minister of Transport and Communications	Abdullah bin Nasir al-Suwaidi
Minister of Labour and Social Affairs	Ali bin Ahmad al-Ansari

Minister of Public Health	Khalid bin Muhammad al-Mana
Minister of Information	Issa Ghanim al-Kawari

The Council of Ministers of the UAE

*Members of ruling families
**Related to ruler of Abu Dhabi, but not a member of the Al Nahyan family

Prime Minister	SHAIKH RASHID SAID AL MAKTOUM (Dubai)*
Deputy Prime Ministers	SHAIKH MAKTOUM BIN RASHID AL MAKTOUM (Dubai)*
	SHAIKH HAMDAN BIN MUHAMMAD AL NAHYAN* (Abu Dhabi)
Minister of Finance and Industry	SHAIKH HAMDAN BIN RASHID AL MAKTOUM (Dubai)*
Minister of Interior	SHAIKH MUBARAK BIN MUHAMMAD AL NAHYAN (Abu Dhabi)*
Minister of Defence	SHAIKH MUHAMMAD BIN RASHID AL MAKTOUM (Dubai)*
Minister of Economy and Trade	Saif Ali al-Jarwan
Minister of Culture and Information	SHAIKH AHMAD BIN HAMID**
Minister of Communications	Muhammad Said Al-Mulla
Minister of Housing and Public Works	Muhammad Khalifah al-Hindi
Minister of Youth and Education	Faraj Fadhil al-Mazroui
Minister of Oil	Mani Said al-Utaybah
Minister of Water and Electricity	Humaid Nasir al-Oweiss
Minister of Justice	Abdallah Humaid al-Mazroui
Minister of Public Health	Hamad Abdel Rahman al-Madfa
Minister of Agriculture	Said Muhammad al-Ragabani

Minister of Planning	SHAIKH HUMAID AL MUALLA (Umm al-Qaiwain)*
Minister of Labour and Social Affairs	Khalfan Mahmud al-Roumi
Minister of Islamic Affairs and Awqaf	Shaikh Muhammad bin Hasan al-Khazraji

Ministers of State

Finance and Industry	Ahmad Humaid al-Tayer
Internal Affairs	Hamouda bin Ali al-Dhairi
Cabinet Affairs	Said al-Ghaith
Supreme Council Affairs	SHAIKH ABDEL AZIZ BIN HUMAID AL QASIMI (Ras al-Khaimah)*
Foreign Affairs	Rashid Abdullah al-Nuaimi
Without Portfolio	SHAIKH AHMAD BIN SULTAN AL QASIMI (Sharjah)*

The Council of Ministers of Oman

*Members of the Al bu Said family

Personal Representative of the Sultan	SAYYID THUWAINI BIN SHIHAB*
Deputy Prime Minister for Security and Defence	SAYYID FAHR BIN TAYMUR*
Deputy Prime Minister for Legal Affairs	SAYYID FAHD BIN MAHMUD*
Deputy Prime Minister for Finance and Economy	Qais bin Abdel Munim al-Zawawi
Minister of Culture and National Heritage	SAYYID FAISAL BIN ALI*
Minister of Agriculture and Fisheries	Muhammad bin Abdullah al-Hinai
Minister of Electricity and Water	Khalfan bin Nasir al-Wahaibi
Minister of Justice, Awqaf and Islamic Affairs	Sayyid Hilal bin Ahmad al-Busaidi
Minister of Health	Dr Mubarak bin Salih al-Khadouri
Minister of Oil	Said bin Ahmad al-Shanfari

Minister of Housing	Abdullah bin Saif al-Busaidi
Minister of Communications	Hamoud bin Abdallah al-Harthi
Minister of Education and Youth Affairs	Yahya bin Mahfudh al-Mantheri
Minister of the Interior	Badr bin Saud bin Hareb
Minister of Information	Abdel Aziz bin Muhammad al-Rowas

Ministers of State

Minister of State and Wali of Dhufar	Hilal bin Saud bin Hareb
Minister of Environment and Water Resources	SAYYID SHABIB BIN TAYMUR*
Minister of State for Defence Affairs	Sayyid al-Mtassim bin Hamoud al-Busaidi
Minister of State for Foreign Affairs	Yusif bin Alawi bin Abdallah
Minister of Commerce and Industry	Salim bin Abdallah al-Ghazali
Minister of Social Affairs and Labour	Mustahail bin Ahmad al-Mashini
Minister of Posts, Telegraphs and Telephones	Ahmad bin Suwaidan al-Balushi
Supervision of Cabinet Secretariat	SAYYID FAHD BIN MAHMUD*
Secretary to the Cabinet	Hamoud bin Faisal bin Said

Index